BLACK GOLD
&
HOLY WAR

The Religious Secret
Behind the Petrodollar

BLACK GOLD
&
HOLY WAR

Ishak Ibraham

THOMAS NELSON PUBLISHERS
Nashville • Camden • New York

Copyright © 1983 by Ishak Ibraham

Published in Nashville, Tennessee, by Thomas Nelson, Inc.
and distributed in Canada by Lawson Falle, Ltd.,
Cambridge, Ontario.

Printed in the United States of America.

Library of Congress Cataloging in Publication Data

Ibraham, Ishak.
  Black gold and holy war.

  1. Islam—20th century. I. Title.
BP161.2.I26 1983   297'.09'04   83-22158
ISBN 0-8407-5860-X

Contents

Introduction

On November 4, 1979, militant Iranian students invaded the United States embassy and other offices in Tehran and took fifty-two employees hostage. This act proved to be a dramatic turning point in America's understanding of modern Islam. "This is not a struggle between the United States and Iran," the Ayatollah Khomeini declared. "It is a struggle between Islam and the infidels." In other words, the Western way of life is anti-Islamic and should be viewed as an adversary of the Islamic way of life.

For more than a year there had been a barrage of headlines about the turmoil in Iran—the riots against the shah's regime, Khomeini's return from exile to lead a spiritual revolution, the horror of seemingly endless executions. Then came the hostage crisis. This was something different, striking a raw nerve in the American psyche. In the following days the suspicion deepened that Islam and its zealots were a threat not only to the lives of the hostages, but also to the peace of the world.

"The governments of the world should know that Islam cannot be defeated," Khomeini declared in August after he had thrown out the shah, executed many of his enemies, and inundated Iran with his style of revolution. "Islam will be victorious in all the countries of the world, and Islam and all the teachings of the Qur'an will prevail all over the world." Non-Islamic countries listened with dismay. Cries of, "Who is this Khomeini anyway?" gave way to, "He's a madman" and, "It makes no sense." Of course it didn't—to the uninformed. But to the Muslims it made perfect sense.

Khomeini's call for worldwide Islamic revolution gathered a million ayes. Islamic moderates wished he had not been so fanatically blunt, just as some Arabs strongly support the establishment of a Palestinian state somewhere on the West Bank but, at the same time, are embarrassed by the various terrorist attacks of the Palestine Liberation Organization (PLO).

But the moderates are increasingly in a minority. Muslims, as never before, are affirming their spiritual identity and flexing their political and economic muscles to propagate the Islamic way of life. The spread of Islam today is greater than it has been at any other point in history. Petrodollars and doctrine form an unprecedented power base to broaden its scope and influence. Islam is no longer "over there" in the Eastern hemisphere. Now it is on our doorstep.

Muslims believe they alone have been given the final revelation of God in the Qur'an, and from this sacred book they are called to be the enforcers of God's will. For all its followers, whether moderate or zealot, young or old, religious or secular, Islam carries the harsh, intolerant imperative to convert or conquer unbelievers. To the Muslim idealist there is no room for moderation. The recent political and economic independence of so many Muslim countries is allowing this uncompromising side of Islam to manifest itself on a greater scale throughout the world.

Increasingly Western society will be faced with the challenge of real Islam. Dollars, mosques, weapons, oil, and any other commodity will be used to squeeze the enemy into surrender. Non-Muslims are pawns in the holy war—the objective being to bring the world under the umbrella of Islamic control and thus, finally, to "fulfill God's will for all people."

If we want to understand critical world-embracing events such as the Arab oil embargo and the Iranian revolution, if we want to develop a more intelligent foreign policy for the Middle East or, for that matter, if we want to understand better the impact of petrodollars on our own economy, we need to come to grips with Islam.

What we must come to see is that the political and economic actions of Khomeini, the decisions of the royal family in Saudi Arabia, and the aggressive statements of Libyan strongman Mu'ammer Qadhafi and the other Islamic leaders are rooted in Islam. The Lebanese war can only be explained in terms of Muslims who are unwilling to tolerate Christian leadership of an Arab country. Muslims must dominate—hence, the civil war. Most Westerners, steeped in the traditions of a separate church and state, have genuine difficulty comprehending this idea. Conversely, Muslims cannot differentiate between the Western way of life and the Judeo-Christian ethical systems which, though they have greatly influenced our standards and values, are not to be exclusively identified with the whole.

Historically, encounters between Islam and Christianity have never been happy. The result has often been war. Muslims, who confess that there is only one true God and that Muhammad is His only true prophet, view Christians as blasphemers for proclaiming that Jesus Christ is the Son of God. Christians who have some knowledge of Islam regard the religion of Muhammad as the religion of the sword. From a religious perspective Christianity and Islam agree on one fundamental principle—God is the Creator of all things—but beyond that point they differ. They are combatants.

Islamic fundamentalism is not a new trend; it is not something that has blossomed in the last ten years. Landrum R. Bolling, writing in the *Saturday Evening Post* (Sept. 1980), makes this clear:

Islam, like other great religions, has had recurring periods of revivalism, interrupted by periods of quietism, decline and decay. The Muslim religion is now, evidently, entering another period of revival and renewal—and of assorted challenges to its non-Islamic neighbors. . . . This is a many faceted movement, with many different leaders and varying objectives. Khomeini did not start it and his passing will not stop it.

Having been born in Egypt, I have experienced firsthand the conflict between Christian and Islamic ways of life. I have written this book for those who want to know more about Islam and its modern approach to its old dream of conquering the world.

Let me add that what I seek to expose in this book is the aggressive, domination-oriented ideology of Islam. I do not hate any individual Muslim. Indeed, as our Lord commanded, I strive to love every person with the love of Christ, and nothing would please me more than to see the Muslim world turn to Him in saving faith. But Islam as a system of thought is a resolutely combative religion, and it is this aspect of Islam that this book examines.

Recent reports have shown that OPEC income is down considerably over that of the previous few years because of the worldwide recession and an attendant reduction in demand for oil. Experts are uncertain about when demand will go up again, by how much, what effect it will have on price, and so on.

I want to emphasize that the principles discussed in this book *are permanent in nature*. Therefore, a temporary gain or loss in income will not in any way slow down the Islamic world in its drive to carry out its mission of chipping away at the Christian's heartland, which Muslims perceive to be their number one rival. One must not think that the Islamic vision for a holy war will be affected by external circumstances such as the price of oil, although the black gold will go a long way toward accomplishing that mission.

1

On Western Doorsteps

The instability the Middle East has experienced for the past few years has pushed it into the limelight of the Western media. As a result, people in the West have become aware of some aspects of the Middle East, but they have not yet begun to understand the heart of the Middle East—Islam.

Regional instability has little effect upon the final mission of Islam, which is to control and convert the world. Should the radical Muslim movement abate, the threat to the Western way of life would not be diminished, for the moderate nations of Islam are the ones who condemn Western materialism and spend billions of dollars in their efforts to convert the West and bring it under their control. Should the radical movement succeed in gaining control in any of the major oil-producing nations, the danger to the West will become more obvious and more immediate than it already is.

In a world economy dependent on oil, countries fortunate enough to possess a superabundance of the coveted black gold can become fantastically wealthy almost overnight. This is precisely what happened with the Arab oil-producing nations. If oil dependency had a negative effect on the world in general, quite the opposite impact was felt by the nations belonging to the Organization of Petroleum Exporting Countries (OPEC). Their staggering profits skyrocketed from $50 billion in 1974 to $200 billion in 1980, and they were projected to reach $1 trillion by 1983. In 1981, Saudi Arabia alone earned $110 billion from the sale of oil.

What are the Arabs doing with all that money? Sensational headlines in the world press seem to indicate that the nouveau riche oil barons have nothing better to do with it than indulge their whims. Stories abound about Saudi Arabian princes casually gambling away millions of dollars at European casinos in a single evening, or more specifically, about the Arab sheik trying to buy the Alamo as a birthday present for his son. These tales are outrageous and amusing but are exceptions to the actual way the bulk of Arab oil profits are used.

The sparsely populated Arab member states in OPEC invested enormous amounts of money in domestic development programs, but they soon ran out of such uses for the vast sums pouring into their treasuries. These states reacted accordingly. The money coming in was channeled immediately into foreign investments, primarily in oil-consuming nations. As an example, Saudi Arabia is now estimated to have $150 billion invested in other countries.

The largest portion of surplus oil money has been invested in the West—mostly in the United States. Publicity surrounding various Arab purchases of foreign land and business is often misleading since it generally focuses on localized issues and, therefore, does not reveal the full extent of Arab investment.

It is impossible to determine accurately the scope of Arab foreign investment because most of it is carefully concealed behind a deliberate screen of secrecy established through third party negotiations. And since the United States government does not know how much Arab money is involved in its economy, it has not yet developed an adequate system to either identify or control those investments.

The Kuwaitis, with their 4.9 percent ownership of some of America's top firms, have holdings just below the level at which disclosure to the United States Securities and Exchange Commission is required. At least two American administrations—that of Gerald Ford and that of Jimmy Carter—were nervous enough about Arab investments to refuse publication of incisive analyses of Arab holdings in the United States. During both administrations, the White House claimed that disclosure would scare off other Arab investors.

To those who are knowledgeable, this Arabic economic offensive is even more alarming than the crisis originating with the oil embargo of 1973. Judith Miller, *New York Times* economic reporter, contends that the oil embargo was at least a

> direct confrontation, something this nation could cope with if it had the wit and the will. The rise in Arab investments . . . is more insidious: if the oil embargo was the stick, the investments are the carrot—some would say drug, on which the nation has become increasingly dependent.

Arab investments are diversified in the United States. American Telephone and Telegraph and its subsidiaries have made use of Arab money to the tune of at least $650 million in loans from the Saudi Arabian Monetary Agency. But Arab investors have also put their money in American real estate, apartments, hotels, shopping centers, tourist resorts and lands, banks, and other financial institutions.

Arab investors constantly seek new investment opportunities in America. Through Kuwait, for example, the Arabs attempted to set up loans for Lockheed, the financially troubled United States aerospace giant. That company turned away from the Arabs when an agreement could not be reached assuring that the Middle Easterners would not control the corporation. The Arabs also pursued American Motors when it was preparing to ask the United States government for loan guarantees totaling $109 million. According to some financial insiders, this sort of maneuvering goes on all the time, although only one out of one hundred such attempts is ever exposed to the public. Nevertheless, a lot of investment hunting is under way.

Some influential Americans help with this investment hunting. Frederick G. Dutton, an assistant secretary of state in the Kennedy administration, has been a consultant for the Saudi Arabian government. Clark Clifford, a former secretary of defense and presidential advisor, is partner in a law firm that is employed by the Algerian government. J. William Fulbright, at one time the chairman of the Senate Foreign Relations Committee, became associated with a law firm listed as an agent for the United Arab Emirates and Saudi Arabia.

That former United States government figures are consultants for Arab governments is no surprise. Much of the OPEC investment in America is in the United States government itself. From 1974 to 1977, OPEC put 34 percent of its total American investment in United States Treasury securities; that amounted to $15 billion. Today this figure is estimated to be twenty or even thirty times higher.

Such high investment levels inevitably lead to the question of potential Arab pressure on the United States to alter policy on critical issues. At what point could Arab governments make threats of financial disruption that, if carried out, would severely damage the economies of the United States and other Western nations? What pressure might be brought to bear on companies doing business with, or largely owned by, Arab governments to use their influence to help bring about decisions favorable to the Arabs?

Take the case of the Flour Corporation in Irvine, California. The company was involved in a $5 billion natural gas conservation project in Saudi Arabia when J. Robert Flour, the company's chairman, asked his stockholders and employees to support a Middle East arms package the Arabs wanted—a package proposed by the Carter administration.

Students of Islam understand that Arab investments are guided more by religious motivations than by capitalistic impulses. Princeton economist Charles Issawy notes that "there is simply a lot of money in the Islamic oil countries now, and they will try to apply Koranic principles when possible in using it."

The Muslim Ummah

Ummah is the Islamic concept of the "community of believers." Some Islamic experts see it as the foundation on which a Muslim common market could be established. If Europe can have its common market, why not the Arab states? Again, the danger lies in the nature of Islam itself.

Europe's common market exists for trade, not as a religious and political tool to convert, subjugate, or eliminate those not in accord.

Already many Muslim nations are uniting economically for the sake of the *Ummah.* At the heart of Muslim investment strategy is the vast international banking system the Arab OPEC nations are building currently. The practically unlimited financial resources of Arab nations, coupled with all Western nations' increasing dependency upon Arab money, give the Arabs a potential stranglehold over the West's economic destiny.

The Arabs threaten to capture control of the world's financial resources in the 1980s in the same way they took control of the world's energy resources in the 1970s. The danger is that development of the Arab banking system could mean a politicizing of international banking in a way that works against the interests of the West.

It is because of the close relationships between the components of the Arab banking system and the Arab states themselves that such politicizing takes place. United States corporations, such as American Telephone and Telegraph, International Business Machines, Dow Chemical, and Kimberly-Clark, have received hundreds of millions of dollars in loans from the Saudi Arabian Monetary Agency. In those cases, that agency functions both as a bank and a facet of the Saudi Arabian treasury.

Kuwait also has its investment bank—the

Kuwait Investment Office. In the early 1980s it tried to buy 15 percent of Getty Oil for $15 billion. In doing so, it acted as an arm of the nation of Kuwait itself, just as it did when it bought 4.9 percent (as much as it could without having to announce its ownership publicly) of virtually all the United States' top twenty banks, plus sizable slices of Eastern Air Lines, Mobil, and Exxon.

As mentioned earlier, both the Ford and Carter administrations were cautious about providing detailed analyses of Arab ownership of businesses in the United States. Any head of state would be cautious if, in disclosing such facts, he enabled the populace to understand the significance of the financial bondage associated with such business dealings. Arabs are demanding, and getting, a voice in running some Western businesses. One European banker observes, "It took the Arabs ten years to learn how to wield their oil power, but it isn't going to take that long to wield their money power."

Islamic centers are springing up all over the West. Mirza Khizar Bakht, secretary-general of the First Interest-Free Finance Consortium, Great Britain's very own Islamic bank, dreams of establishing a Muslim shopping center in central London, in Regent Street, or in Knightsbridge. The aim of the center would be to "unite the whole Muslim world in London."

Mirza Khizar Bakht's notion of London as a center of Islam is becoming a reality. The Islamic Council of Europe, based in London, spends large sums on propaganda among Muslims and Christians and wants to build mosques in each major European city. Already the Central Mosque in London raises its minaret into the English sky. Built at an estimated cost of $7.5 million, it seats 2,800 people.

While London is a base of operations for expansion, the greatest number of European Muslims lives on the Continent. France has a Muslim population of over 2 million. West Germany follows with 1.7 million, and the number there is expanding as Islamic centers and schools are established. In Spain, leftists and environmentalists find it fashionable to be Muslim. In Rome, a new mosque is being constructed at an estimated cost of $20 million.

The Ummah *in the United States*

The erection of Islamic mosques and the propagation of Islamic teachings are being pursued vigorously in the United States. Muslims recently purchased a thousand acres near Abiquiu, New Mexico, to build a model city of Islam. The town will house one hundred families and will include a seven-domed adobe mosque, a school, and a literature center. Saudi Arabia and other Muslim countries are spending tens of millions of dollars in community development and other projects throughout the United States. Their aim is to help the Muslim communities expand.

It is estimated that in the 1970s Islam grew by 400 percent in the United States. Many Americans, predominantly blacks, are turning to Islam to reject values and ideals they consider to be outgrowths of a hypocritical white Christian society. When one black Muslim was asked why he had turned to Islam, he answered, "Christianity is a racist religion; Islam is the religion of peace." As contrary to historical fact as this statement may be, the thought has become dominant in the minds of many black Americans.

The black Muslims in the United States have begun to integrate themselves actively into the wider community of Orthodox Islam, and the American movement has taken the title of "World Community of Islam in the West." Black Muslim Americans historically have not been recognized by Orthodox Islam because of their belief in black supremacy and "other heresies." But under their present leader, Elijah Mohammed, Jr., black Muslims are working to come to a meeting of the minds with the leadership of Orthodox Islam. Muslims in America number between two and three million, a figure that is increasing rapidly.

Muslim membership in America comes from two sources—converts and immigrants. American converts to Islam seem to fall largely within the twenty- to thirty-year-old age group. They are mainly black Americans from lower income brackets. But an American church official estimates that 70,000 Caucasians have turned to Islam between 1973 and 1983.

Since the late sixties, several important Islamic organizations have arisen in the United States. Those organizations exist to strengthen and support American Muslims and to propagate their message and the practice of their faith. The Council of Imams trains local mosque prayer leaders, and the Association of Muslim Students has at least two hundred active chapters on United States college campuses. Those groups have their equivalents in England, Australia, and other Western countries.

A brochure sent out from the headquarters of the Association of Muslim Students in Plainfield, Indiana, describes the group's five top priorities as follows: (1) disseminating Islam through publications geared to both Muslims and non-Muslims; (2) establishing Islamic institutions, including places of worship, community service centers, and educational facilities; (3) assisting Muslims in practical aspects of religious observance (the five pillars of Islam); (4) propagating and facilitating Islam's faith-sharing effort among non-Muslims; and (5) encouraging the "unity of Muslim conscience" through a heightened sense of belonging and Muslim identity. With vast sums of money at their disposal, there is no doubt that Islamic Americans will be able to spread their message far and wide in the United States.

Few people realize just how aggressive Islamic missions in the West are. Great Britain seems to be a special target for Islam. One Muslim leader declares that the United Kingdom is "ripe for conversion." There are now over three hundred mosques in Great Britain; some of them are former Christian churches. Also, Great Britain has twenty-two English-language newspapers that propagate Islamic teaching by various methods.

In 1976, the world's first Festival of Islam was held in England. It was opened by the Queen, and it lasted three months. The festival statement declared, "Unless we win London over to Islam, we will fail to win the whole of the Western world." As part of the festival, a missionary training center was opened, and Islam's intentions were made clear in a London press conference, which was headlined, "Muslims Launch Missionary Crusade for Britain and the Rest of the World."

What Does It All Mean?

This chapter has provided an overview of two relatively recent and potentially very dangerous phenomena: (1) the investment of billions of Arab dollars in the American economy, and (2) the pouring of huge sums of money into aggressive

Islamic evangelistic efforts here in the West. The danger in the first case is that as Arab investment grows, our economy increasingly will be dependent on their money and vulnerable to disruption by them.

The danger in the second case is perhaps more subtle, but its consequences could be even more devastating. We in the United States enjoy religious freedom, and people of all faiths, including Islam, are at liberty to practice their religion and evangelize. But every person placing his trust in Islam rather than in Jesus Christ is lost eternally. If the followers of Islam are increasing their efforts to win the hearts and minds of the world, we must redouble our own efforts to reach the world with the gospel of Jesus Christ. By the same token, most Arab Islamic nations consider Christian missions to be a crime, and they are punished as such.

2

OPEC and Islam

In the late twentieth century, the religion of Muhammad has blended with a new and powerful uprising of Arab nationalism. As a result, Islam has become not only the symbol of Arab culture, but also a potent expression of anti-Western sentiment. Couple this with the disturbing fact that oil-consuming nations are becoming subservient to wealthy, oil-producing nations, and the economic forecast for the West is not optimistic.

Nations who are beneficiaries of Arab money and aid must begin to take seriously Islamic religious influence and its imposition of conditions for the use of that money. Islam says that no Muslim should be answerable to a non-Muslim. What would happen, then, to a company whose controlling interest was suddenly owned by Muslims? Would the top management be replaced with Muslim personnel who would be accountable only to one another? Or suppose an American company demanded that its personnel convert to Islam to win a Middle Eastern contract? Too far-fetched, you say? Is it? There are signals that Western institutions are already acceding to Islamic demands in order to capture Arab petrodollars.

The West, which makes a keen separation between business and religious activities, is generally ignorant of the close links between OPEC'S controlling leadership and Islam. A small but growing number of Westerners, however, are having their ignorance rudely dispelled by harsh experience.

Wade Kern, for instance, understands this link very well. Kern, an airplane pilot and a Southern Baptist, sued Dynaelectron Corporation of McLean, Virginia, for firing him—allegedly because he would not convert to Islam. Dynaelectron, an engineering company, had won a contract to work at the Sacred Mosque in Mecca, Saudi Arabia. Thirty employees, on orders from the Saudi government, became Muslims so that they could man firefighting helicopters during pilgrimages to the mosque. Kern refused to bend to the Saudi insistence that he become a Muslim— the reason, he contends, that he lost his job.

Moreover, Islamic nations have little reluctance about entering alliances with any of their brethren simply on the strength of the Muslim bond, no matter how questionable, even sinister, those alliances might be. Idi Amin, former infamous ruler of Uganda, slaughtered an estimated 300,000 Christians and, when overthrown, slipped out of Uganda into the protective arms of his Muslim brothers in Libya and Saudi Arabia.

As the Arabs continue their massive investments in the West, they desperately want to avoid disclosure of their huge holdings in United States Treasury bills and bonds. Why? First, the more moderate countries, such as Saudi Arabia and Kuwait, recoil at the fanaticism of the hardline Muslim states such as Libya and Iran. Generally, they feel that the less radicals know about their business dealings, the better off they are. Second, the Arab investors do not want the West to panic over an apparent Muslim economic invasion and thus jeopardize their own economic interests.

Stanley Reed, a specialist in Middle Eastern affairs, recently wrote about the Arab infatuation with keeping their investments cloaked: "Why this great penchant for secrecy?" Peter Iseman, an American Arabist and repository of desert lore, says, "They never want to tell how much gold they have under the mattress."

> The Arabs also sense that their great new wealth has made them enemies and perhaps increased their vulnerability. "The Saudis and Kuwaitis want people to think they are very poor," explains an executive who specializes in liaison with Arabian officials. "They want them to think they have only enough money for a few days."[1]

---

[1] *Barron's National Business and Financial Weekly* (Sept. 13, 1982).

Muslim Influence

It is not unreasonable to expect Muslim countries to flex their economic muscles in the international political arena. In the Middle East itself, radical states such as Iraq, Libya, and Syria probably will combine political and financial resources in order to influence the moderate Arab nations. If that does not work, there is always the potential of fundamentalist Muslim countries trying to spark regime-toppling revolutions in the more stable Arab states.

Actually, the Muslim zone of influence, far from being limited to the Middle East, is already worldwide. The use of economic-political muscle was evident in the bid for observer status for the Palestine Liberation Organization at meetings of the International Monetary Fund (IMF) and the World Bank. Such tactics had already been used successfully by some Arab states against the IMF in 1977 when Saudi Arabia won permanent seating on the IMF board, a step that represented a significant shift in IMF policy for Third World involvement.

Western economic dependence on oil opens the door to Arab, and therefore Islamic, influence and control. OPEC began using the oil weapon in 1973 as a punitive measure against countries that supported Israel in the Yom Kippur War. That was merely the beginning of what promises to become a master economic and political strategy, undergirded by religious conviction, for promoting Islamic interests throughout the world.

The United States is the world's largest importer of foreign oil. As much as some American economists would like to deny it, their country has become dependent on a system which, to a great degree, can subject the world's strongest economy to its own desires and whims. By the mid-1970s, the United States was importing an average of 8.67 million barrels of oil per day, which represented 47 percent of its oil needs. A decade earlier, imported oil comprised only 12 percent of America's daily requirements.

In the 1980s, the picture is basically the same. The tragedy is that the United States is still so dependent on OPEC oil—despite press attention focused on her dangerous addiction, despite the creation of a Department of Energy (which was later disassembled), and despite efforts at conservation. In 1960, John F. Kennedy inspired the United States to soar beyond earth's gravitational pull to the moon. But two decades later, no American president has been able to challenge his nation successfully to leap out of OPEC's gravitational barrier to energy independence.

The impact of American dependence on OPEC oil has a worldwide effect. Roy Werner, assistant to United States Senator John Glenn, stated that "continuing high demand by the United States market has been a major factor in keeping OPEC prices high." In fact, following the OPEC oil embargo of 1973, and a resulting 366 percent increase in oil prices, the world energy bill rose from $20 billion in 1973 to $100 billion in 1976. That exorbitant cost dealt harshly with many of the world's major economies. There was a loss of half a million jobs and a worldwide decrease of GNP amounting to nearly $20 billion.

Three Islamic Convictions

To understand the relationship between OPEC and Islam, one must come to grips with the Islamic mind and three burning convictions that stem from it. The *first* is that economic success demonstrates God's pleasure. Prior to the development of the world's thirst for oil, Muslims measured Allah's blessing by the standards of the battlefield. Beginning with the Battle of Badr in A.D. 624, victories in war became proof of divine support. That conviction deepened during Islam's first century as its conquest spread over the Middle East, North Africa, and as far west as Spain. Since the first Arabic converts believed that Islam was the religion by which Allah revealed the weaknesses of all other faiths, they were convinced that Muslim victories validated their cause.

Today Islam interprets financial success as evidence of Allah's blessing on all Islamic advances. This explains why moderate Muslims, although embarrassed with Khomeini's excesses during the Iranian revolution, would not totally disown him.

Khomeini may speak the truth too bluntly, they feel, but he does speak the truth for most Muslims.

The *second* conviction relates to the flow of black gold. Oil is Allah's gift to Muslims so that they may achieve superiority, thus proving the supremacy of Islam and enabling the subjugation of all other religions, their adherents, and the societies where they flourish. J. B. Kelly, author of *Arabia, the Gulf and the West*, noted that as a result of

> powerful sentiments of grievance and resentment against the West, the Arabs see the oil weapon as a gift sent by God to redress the balance between Christendom and Islam . . . and to fulfill the destiny which God in His infinite wisdom has ordained for those to whom He has chosen to reveal the one true faith. Extravagant though these fancies may appear to Western eyes, they are very real to those who entertain them, and infinitely more appealing than the calmer dictates of reason.[2]

The fact that most of the OPEC oil controllers are Muslims (with some exceptions such as Venezuela and Nigeria) brings us to the *third* burning conviction welding together OPEC and Islam: Arab culture is the ideal expression of Islam. "I cannot see Arab culture separate from Islamic culture," said Algeria's Ben Bella. "I honestly

---

[2]J. B. Kelly, "Islam Through the Looking Glass," *The Heritage Lectures* (Washington: The Heritage Foundation, 1980), p. 8.

would not understand the meaning of Arab culture if it were not first and foremost Islamic." But the matter is deeper than that. If there is cultural imperialism related to Islam, it is the imperialism that runs so deep that the Muslims believe the Qur'an can be in one language only—Arabic. Translations into languages other than Arabic are not considered to be the genuine Qur'an, but merely interpretations.

This belief explains the anger fanatic Muslims feel when their Arab countrymen appear to adopt certain Western cultural patterns. One of the frustrations shared by the Muslim Brotherhood and the Iranian Muslim extremists was that many people in their societies adopted Western modes of dress and preferred Western styles of entertainment. The issue, in the minds of fundamentalist Muslims, had nothing to do with whether particular elements of Western lifestyle were desirable or objectionable. The important point to those Muslims was simply that Western cultural attire is not Arabic, and only Arabic culture can be the pure expression of Islam.

This is one of many reasons why Islam has no doctrine of separation of church and state. Because of close identification with one culture and the need to maintain that culture as an expression of Islam, religion and society are merged. Imam Mohammed Jawad Chirri, the leader of Detroit's Islamic Center, observed that "with the advent of Khomeini, Muslims discovered that an Islamic state is workable, a religious state is better for everybody." Such a philosophy grows from the desire of Muhammad himself to create a society in which religion encompasses everything.

Muslim extremists demand a society controlled, pervaded, and purged by religion and established on and maintained by Arabic culture. They are willing to use every conceivable force to achieve this so-called "Divine objective."

The Dhimmi *Mentality*

Islamic law is the core of Islamic thought. In Islamic law systems the Muslim attitude toward non-Muslims becomes most clear. Non-Muslims do not belong to the House of Islam *(Dar al-Islam)*; therefore they are enemies because they belong to the House of War *(Dar al-Harb)*. Although interpreters of Islamic laws have disagreed on the method for implementing this law, there are only three alternatives for dealing with non-Muslims under the Islamic legal system: (1) they must be converted; (2) they must be subjugated; or (3) they must be eliminated (except for women, children, and slaves).

Islamic law, however, distinguishes between non-Muslims. So Christians and Jews, for example, are in different categories from the rest. Thus, some Muslim states will permit the "infidel" to enter a formal agreement or treaty that will spare the unbeliever's life and property. In that case, the non-Muslim becomes a *dhimmi* and is subjugated in various ways. According to Islamic law a *dhimmi* must wear identifiable clothing and live in a clearly marked house. He must not ride a horse or bear arms. He must yield the right-of-way to Muslims. The *dhimmi* cannot be a witness in a legal court except in matters relating to other *dhimmis*. He cannot be the guardian of a Muslim child, the owner of a Muslim slave, or a judge in a Muslim court.[3]

Why mention this apparently insignificant matter? Actually this concept of *dhimmi* is of great significance. It is typical of how Muslims, in interpreting the Qur'an and Islamic law, often take minor concepts and establish major practices affecting Islamic society and economic and political policy based upon them. This *dhimmi* mentality underlies OPEC's relations with non-Muslim nations in the use of its oil resources. While Western countries view petroleum issues as having primarily an economic or political connotation, the Islamic mind is thinking *dhimmi*. Since Muslims believe Islamic superiority can be demonstrated by humiliating the infidel, they must find a means for bringing the unbeliever under subjugation. Oil provides just the means of humiliation and subjugation. Western politicians who hope the oil sheiks will have pity over long gasoline lines and

---

[3]A. S. Tritton, *The Caliphs and Their Non-Muslim Subjects* (London: Frank Cass & Co. 1970).

economy-shattering inflation and unemployment will find their optimism as groundless as the shifting sands of the Sahara's dunes. On the contrary, the inflation and large budget deficits that inconvenience and oppress Western nations and force them to acknowledge dependence on OPEC simply proves to the Islamic oil barons that Allah is with them and Islamic economic policy will prevail.

The New Sword

In the twentieth century, Muslims are using oil the same way they used the sword in the seventh century—as a means of exerting the greatest possible force upon their adversaries. The linkage between OPEC and Islam follows a logical sequence: economic success is the proof of God's favor; this success will result in Islamic superiority; the black gold gives to the Arabs an ideal world state which expresses the true culture of Islam; other religions and cultures must be subjugated; and oil has been given by Allah as the new weapon for controlling the Christian West by humiliating it. Once this is achieved, to their way of thinking at least, defeating atheism (communism) is relatively easy.

Until those from the West who sit with the sheiks at the negotiating table understand the nature of Islam, they will not get to the real root of the oil crisis. The West can flood OPEC countries

with geologists, petroleum engineers, economists, and diplomats, but until such experts see
the linkage between Islam and OPEC, their efforts
will be depressingly futile.

3

The Birth of Islam

As we examine the marriage of Islamic ideology and Arab wealth, it is essential that we understand how Islam began and how it developed into an anti-Western and anti-Christian religion. Looking at this history, we will see how the story of Islam became the story of the Arab world.

Until the seventh century, when the Muslim conquest drew aside the veil of obscurity, Arabia was virtually an unknown land. In A.D. 610, in a cave at the foot of Mount Hira near Mecca (in what is now Saudi Arabia), a man named Ibn Abd Allah from the tribe of Quraish had a vision. As a result, this man and his work transformed the lives of millions of people and affected significantly the history of the modern world.

According to the account of Ibn Ishaq, Muhammad's first biographer, the future prophet was fast asleep when the angel Gabriel appeared and commanded him: "Recite!" Startled and afraid, Muhammad asked, "What shall I recite?" Immediately he felt his throat tighten as if the angel had grabbed his neck and was choking him. "Recite!" the angel again commanded. And Muhammad again felt the angel's mighty grip. "Recite!" the angel commanded for the third time. "Recite in the name of the Lord, the Creator who created man from a clot of blood! Recite! Your Lord is most gracious. It is he who has taught man by the pen that which he does not know."

Thus it happened that Muhammad was inspired to preach the word of Allah and that the first verses of the Qur'an, which literally means "recitation," were revealed to him.

Arab Religion Before Muhammad

A great stream of caravan traders constantly passed through the Arabian peninsula, making it the commercial land-link between the Mediterranean and the Far East. Trade grew until, by the middle of the sixth century, there were three major towns in northern Arabia. Mecca was by far the most important and prosperous of these, and by Muhammad's time it was quite a bustling city.

Mecca was also a religious center. Pilgrims went there from far and wide to worship at the Kaaba, Arabia's holiest pagan shrine. The Arabs of the region had a faith deep-rooted in idolatry. For centuries they had stood aloof from every attempt by Christians from Syria and Egypt to convert them. Each of the nomadic Bedouin tribes living in the vast Arabian desert worshiped a variety of deities and nature spirits of its own, but some gods were revered in common. The Kaaba was the shrine of these commonly acknowledged deities, all of whom Muhammad would expel when he established the Kaaba as the central shrine of the new religion of Islam.

Two factors combined to make Arabia unusually resistant to the spread of the Christian gospel. The idolatry practiced in Mecca before the establishment of Islam was a compromise with Judaism, and it had introduced enough legends to steel the mind against Christianity. Also, Christianity of the seventh century was itself corrupt and decrepit, beset as it was by all kinds of heresies and schisms, particularly regarding the nature of Christ. The New Testament was respected, if not revered, as a book that claimed to be the revealed Word of God, but the few Christians in Arabia had embraced a lackluster Christianity. Thus, Christianity as practiced in Arabia held no appeal for most of the people there.

The tenets of Judaism, however, were widely familiar to the Arabians through Jewish legends. To some extent, worship at the Kaaba was founded on Jewish patriarchal traditions common to Christianity as well. Thus, the ground Muhammad planted with Islam was a wide, fertile field, bordering the truth in some places.

The material for a great transformation of religious consciousness in Arabia was there, but it needed molding and shaping. Muhammad was the workman. Had Muhammad, stern in his early convictions, followed the leading of Christian truth there might have been in Christian history a Saint Muhammad—more likely, Muhammad the Martyr—laying the foundation stone of the Arabian church.

Abraham and Islam

Legend attributes the building of the Kaaba to Abraham. The story goes that as Hagar was wandering in the desert with her young son, Ishmael, they reached Mecca almost dying of thirst. While Hagar was looking for water between two hills, Ishmael waited in the shade of a tree. Then, as Ishmael cried out with thirst, small bubbles under his feet became a stream of sweet, flowing water. The place where the water is believed to have first appeared is known as the well of Zemzem, which still gives water today. The legend continues that on a subsequent visit to Zemzem, Abraham was to offer his son as a sacrifice, but he was stopped by God. Abraham, assisted by his son, then built the Kaaba at God's command. However, Jews who lived in Arabia at the time refused to participate in the pagan worship at the Kaaba, refuting the story as myth by claiming that Abraham never came as far as Mecca. Now this "holy place" is the focal point of Islamic worship.

Basing his claim on the legend of the Kaaba, Muhammad sought to legitimize his new religion. He argued that Islam's relationship to Abraham made it the equal of Judaism and Christianity. Later in his life, however, he revised this claim, stating that his revelation superseded both Judaism and Christianity and had become the final revelation of God.

The Life of the Prophet

Born in Mecca in the autumn of A.D. 570, Muhammad was given his name, a rare one among Arabs which means "highly praised," by his mother and his grandfather. His father, a trader named Abdullah, died before Muhammad was born. According to the custom of Meccan aristocracy, the infant Muhammad was sent to the desert to be wet-nursed by a Bedouin mother. Muhammad spent most of his childhood years with the nurse Halima, among the Beni Saad tribesmen. When Muhammad was four, Halima discovered that he was suffering from a form of epilepsy, but this illness was kept secret at the time because of superstition regarding demon possession. Some of his followers later interpreted Muhammad's epilepsy as a form of inspiration.

At age five Muhammad was returned to his mother, but she became ill and died. His care was then the responsibility of Abdul Muttalib, his grandfather, who loved Muhammad devotedly.

Unfortunately the grandfather also soon died, and Abu Talib, Muhammad's uncle, took charge of him until his adulthood.

At the age of twelve, Muhammad took his first business trip to Syria with Abu Talib. It was a several-month journey filled with a multitude of rich experiences that were not wasted upon Muhammad. They passed through Jewish settlements and came in contact with the Christians in Syria. No doubt he saw the churches, the crosses, and the images and symbols of their faith.

Muhammad was exposed, in still another important way, to the winds of religious debate blowing through the Middle East in the seventh century. At the annual fairs in Mecca, Christian as well as Jewish poets and theologians would gather to recite their poetry or preach the essence of their faith to the gathered crowds.

The influence of Judaism and Christianity upon Muhammad was in form only, however, and did not give him a genuine understanding of either doctrine. Muhammad showed far more familiarity with Judaism than with Christianity, most likely because Judaism was much more prominent in the area. But one thing Muhammad understood clearly was the disdainful way in which Christians and Jews regarded each other and how both spurned the Arab tribes as heathens bound to receive the wrath of an offended God.

Very little else is known about Muhammad's teen years. Like other lads, he tended the sheep and goats of Mecca in the neighboring hills and valleys. Authorities agree that he was respected for his thoughtful nature and his integrity; he was nicknamed al-Amin, "the trustworthy." He must have lived a quiet, peaceful life with the family of Abu Talib.

At twenty-five, traveling the same route he had trekked thirteen years earlier with his uncle, Muhammad led a caravan expedition to Syria for a widow named Khadija. There Muhammad lost no time delving into the practices of the Syrian Christians and conversing with the monks and clergy he met. He spoke of them with respect and even praise in the Qur'an. For their doctrine, though, he had no sympathy because of his misunderstanding of the true teachings of Christ.

It is possible that the picture of Christianity in the Qur'an was painted, in some considerable degree, from impressions formed on this journey. It is also possible that in the sincerity of his early search after the truth, he might have readily embraced, and faithfully adhered to, the teaching of Jesus. But, as Sir William Muir said,

> instead of the simple message of the Gospel as a revelation of God reconciling mankind unto Himself through His son, the sacred dogma of the trinity was forced upon the traveler with . . . offensive zeal . . . and the worship of Mary was exhibited in so gross a form as to leave the impression in Muhammad's mind that she was

held to be a goddess if not the third person of the trinity.[1]

Add to this the ancient Arab pagan belief that the gods could have sexual intercourse with human women, producing children called the sons of God, and it is understandable that Muhammad rejected what he thought to be the Christian teaching. Far be it from the holy God to produce Jesus through sexual intercourse with a human. Thus, Muhammad refused to call Jesus the Son of God, choosing instead to call Him the son of Mary.

Upon returning from that first commercial expedition, which proved to be very successful financially, Muhammad married Khadija. She was fifteen years older and had been married twice before. Although Muhammad would have nine other wives and countless concubines after her death, he had none but Khadija while she lived. In turn, she gave him unfailing support when he began preaching to the Meccans a message they did not want to hear. She also bore Muhammad two sons and a daughter.

Muhammad Finds His Mission

As he approached forty, Muhammad spent more and more time pondering the question

---

[1]Sir William Muir, *The Life of Mohammed* (Edinburgh: John Grant, 1923).

"What is truth?" His soul was perplexed, especially by the social injustice he saw even among the clans in his own tribe.

Muhammad's clan was the poorer group of the two main clans in the tribe of Quraish. Naturally he was distressed to watch the rival clan grow rich and strong while his own grew weaker. One of his aims was to create a more just social system that would protect the poor, the widows, and the orphans, and would replace the existing system in which the strong abused the weak.

Thus burdened, Muhammad frequently meditated in solitude in the countryside near Mecca; a favorite spot was a cave about two or three miles to the north. One day his contemplation and search were over—the day of his disturbing and fateful vision—and he returned from his solitude telling Khadija that God had commissioned him to preach. She lost no time in consulting her *hanif* kinsman, a holy man who listened to the story and unhesitatingly declared that Muhammad had been chosen, like Moses, to receive divine inspiration and to be the prophet of his people.

The Muslims insist that Muhammad was illiterate. This, of course, substantiates his claim to have received his revelations directly from Allah. Muslims consider Muhammad's sacred vision and the subsequent recitation which makes up the Qur'an to be miraculous acts of God. Muhammad himself, however, worked no miracles, and Islam vehemently asserts the ordinary humanity of the prophet. Muslims do not like to be called Muham-madans because it implies that they worship Muhammad as Christians worship Christ.

Even before his first revelation, Muhammad had earned a reputation for being a wise and saintly man. According to legend, Muhammad looked out from his balcony one day to see members of four clans engaged in dispute over which one of them would carry the Black Stone, which the pagan Arabs regarded as sacred, to its new niche in the Kaaba. Muhammad successfully resolved the argument to everyone's satisfaction by propos-ing a compromise. He instructed each tribe to lift one corner of a blanket upon which he placed the meteorite, and he personally set the Black Stone in its resting place, where it remains today.

During the period following his initial revela-tion, Muhammad received no further messages from God, and he began to become fearful and depressed, even to the point of considering suicide. That period is thought to have lasted anywhere from six months to three years. However, the accounts are confused and some-times contradictory. We can only conclude that there was a season during which Muhammad's mind was confused, and he was uncertain of himself and his mission.

Some unproven traditions might explain that period. Waraqa ibn Naufal, Khadija's cousin, was a Christian scholar who, we are told, translated portions of the New Testament into Hebrew and

Arabic. Waraqa was tutoring Muhammad in the Christian faith, but after only a short time Waraqa died, leaving Muhammad in confusion. With no help available to relieve his frustration, Muhammad decided to go his own way alone.

Muhammad's own account of his revelation is worth noting. "Inspiration," he said,

> cometh in one of two ways; sometimes Gabriel communicateth the revelation to me, as one man to another, and this is easy; at other times, it is like the ringing of a bell, penetrating my very heart, and rending me; and this it is which afflict-eth me the most.

Muhammad and the Jews of Arabia

By the time he was forty-four, Muhammad had emerged from doubt and obscurity. He asserted unequivocally that he was ordained a prophet with a commission to the people of Arabia, reciting his warnings and exhortations and messages as coming directly from God. He taught that Allah was the one God and that men must thank him for their existence and worship him only. He preached equality before God and justice among men, and warned that because man's destiny was in God's hands, there would be a Day of Judgment for all men. His wife Khadija was his first convert, followed by his slave Zaid, whom he later adopted as his son. Then followed two of his most trusted

49

friends, Abu Bakr and Umar, who later succeeded him as leaders of the Muslim movement. But in Mecca, Muhammad met with stiff opposition from his own tribe; they refused to acknowledge him as a prophet and refused to give up idol worship.

During the early years of his mission, Muhammad developed a close relationship with the Jews. Some acknowledged him to be the prophet, the messiah, descended from Abraham. The majority of Jews, however, maintained a "wait and see" policy. Muhammad, in turn, incorporated into the new religion many Jewish traditions and numerous Old Testament stories. Those include, as we saw earlier, the story of Abraham's offering his son for a sacrifice, the story of Hagar and Ishmael, stories about Joseph and Jacob, and the account of the destruction of Sodom and Gomorrah. In the Qur'an, those stories are usually mixed with other (fictional) incidents.

Muhammad's attempt to turn the hearts of the Meccans proved frustrating and unsuccessful. Mecca enjoyed a religious society that was closely connected with its commercial activity, and it proved to be a closed society into which Muhammad was unable to penetrate.

Discouraged, Muhammad and his followers went to the city of Medina in a mass migration known in Islamic history as the *hijra*. In Medina, Muhammad struck a much more responsive chord in the people's hearts. The city harbored a large community of Jews who endlessly threatened the pagans with the coming Messiah as revenge for the injustice inflicted upon them. This situation made the population ready to accept Muhammad's message, and they were more prepared for monotheistic religious ideas than were the worldly Meccans.

That sociopolitical arrangement provided Muhammad with the perfect opportunity to bring Jews and pagans together under the banner of Allah. In doing so, he tried to please the Jews by adopting some of their religious rites. The Jewish Day of Atonement became the Muslim fast day of Ashura. Prayer was increased from two to three times (later to five times) daily to accommodate the Jewish midday prayer. Muslims held a public service, such as the Jews had in synagogues, with Friday equal to the Jewish sabbath. And Muhammad adopted the Jewish call to prayer, but instead of the trumpet of the Jews, Muhammad used a human prayer-caller *(muezzin)*.

Subsequently, when disputes with the Jews occurred, Jewish opposition and rejection of his message disappointed and angered Muhammad. He, in turn, accused the Jews of rejecting the truth and claimed Jewish property for his own private ownership.

Muhammad never seemed to show the same interest in the Christian faith. Nor did he have the same opportunity to learn its history and doctrines. However, his attitude toward Christianity was just as favorable as it had been toward

Judaism. At no time was his dialogue with Christians embittered by causes similar to those which led eventually to his hostile relationship with the Jews. But Muhammad's relationship with the Christian faith never advanced significantly beyond the point at which it is described in the Qur'an.

Muhammad's mission followed a pattern of development that might be called "progressive revelation." He started out to warn and reform the pagan society of the Arabian peninsula, asking people to turn to the true God, the God of Abraham. Then, equating his revelation with that of Judaism and Christianity, he perceived himself to be on equal footing with Moses and Jesus. Finally, he saw himself and his message as the final word of God that superseded both previous religions.

This progression brought him to believe that Islam was the universal faith, the faith that started with Abraham (the first Muslim according to Muhammad). Muhammad believed that, because Jews and Christians had moved away from God's intended purpose, God had to send him to proclaim the ultimate revelation. In his own mind at least, Muhammad rose triumphant over both the Law and the gospel. The new message of Allah was announced in the Arabic language and intended for Arabs, who henceforth would have a prophet and a holy book of their own.

To Muhammad the Jew was to follow the Law

and the Christian was to hold fast to the gospel. Both Jew and Christian were to admit as equal with their own prophets and Scriptures the apostleship of Muhammad and the authority of the Qur'an.

> Say: O People of the Book! Ye do not stand upon any sure ground until you observe both the Torah and the Gospel as well as that which has been now sent down unto you from your Lord [i.e., the Qur'an] (5:68).

For a short time the Jews remained on cordial terms with their new ally. But it soon became evident that Judaism could not go hand-in-hand with Islam, because Muhammad began to see his mission as more than mere protest against error and superstition. Every day brought Islam closer to being exclusive and demanding a priority status. Ultimately, at his farewell pilgrimage, Muhammad barred Christians and Jews from visiting the Kaaba and by "divine command" declared war against them until they confessed the supremacy of Islam or consented to pay tribute. "Paradise is the reward for those who die in the way of God," he declared, "and the booty is the reward of those who survive the war." While no one can deny the significance of Muhammad's religious conviction, it is evident that Muhammad, in addition to espousing a doctrine, formed a new religious society. To ensure his political preeminence, he advocated warring against non-Muslims to bring them under control. The real importance of this concept lies in the force and the scope of the arena in which it was applied in the post-Muhammad era.

Throughout the Qur'an, Muhammad developed a form of theocratic government pertinent to all departments of life, beginning with the conduct of dissidents, the treatment of allies, the formation of treaties, and other political matters. Later, elements of a code of conduct and moral law were introduced.

Few men have had such impact upon the world as Muhammad. Thirteen centuries after his death, about 700 million people are followers of the religion he founded. Toward the end of his life, Muhammad began to clarify his own aspirations as to the future spread of Islam. He made a silver seal engraved with the words "Muhammad the apostle of God" and sent four simultaneous messages bearing this stamp to the rulers of Egypt, Abyssinia, Syria, and Persia, urging them to forsake their idols and to believe the true universal faith of God's message given through him, God's messenger.

When Muhammad was sixty-three, and Islam was only twenty years old, the "apostle of God" fell ill with a sudden fever and died. As the news of his death spread, the new Muslims were seized with panic and confusion. But Abu Bakr, Muhammad's close friend and later the first Islamic caliph (successor of the Prophet), declared to Muhammad's distraught followers, "Whichever of you worships Muhammad, know that Muhammad is dead. But whichever of you worships God, know that God is alive and does not die." He then quoted a verse from the Qur'an which gains significance with the hindsight of history: "Muhammad is a Prophet only; there have been Prophets before him. If he dies or is slain, will ye turn back?"

Holy War

Even this brief sketch of the spiritual and historical roots of Islam is sufficient to illustrate one of Islam's most powerful concepts—*jihad*, or "holy war." The word literally means "struggle." Not every Muslim would agree that *jihad* requires spilling the blood of infidels, but struggle for the victory of Islam is a factor in the life of every faithful Muslim.

Al-Banna has explained the importance of *jihad* this way:

How wise was the man who said "force is the surest way of implementing the right and how beautiful it is that force and right should march side by side." This striving to broadcast the Islamic mission, quite apart from preserving the hallowed concepts of Islam, is another religious duty imposed by God on the Muslims, just as he imposed fasting, prayer, pilgrimage, alms, and the doing of good and abandonment of evil,

upon them. He imposes it upon them and dele-
gated them to do it. He did not excuse anyone
possessing strength and capacity from performing it. . . .[2]

Jihad, according to Islamic law, is to be waged
until the Day of Judgment—or forever. There may
be times when Muslim armies appear to be
defeated, but even legal armistices can be broken
when it is in the best interests of Islam. But there
can be no possible permanent peace with "infidel
countries." Since superiority is such a vital factor
in Islamic thought, domination of the world is the
only worthy expression of Islam's greatness.

It is not strange, therefore, to read in the Qur'an
that Allah exhorts Muslims not to take Jews or
Christians for friends:

> Oh ye who believe! Take not the Jews and Chris-
> tians for friends. They are friends one to another.
> He among you who taketh them for friends is
> one of them (5:51).

This lack of trust toward any non-Muslim is
prominent throughout the Qur'an:

> Believers do not make friends with anyone other
> than your own people. They desire nothing but
> ruin. Their hatred is clear from what they say, but

---

[2]Hasan Al-Banna, "To What Do We Summon Mankind?",
Five Tracts of Hasan Al-Banna, trans. Charles Wendell
(Berkeley: University of California Press, 1978), p. 80.

more violent is the hatred which their breasts conceal (3:118).

According to Muslim extremists, such Qur'anic texts as the one quoted above enforce this intolerant attitude toward non-Muslims. They also constantly exhort the "faithful" to begin a holy war against Jews, Christians, and other non-Muslims. This teaching makes it virtually impossible for Muslims to interact on a trust basis with anyone who is not a member of the Muslim brotherhood.

Islamic "superiority" reaches its apex in the Qur'an in chapter 5, verse 33. There, Muslims are commanded to fight non-Muslims and anyone who rejects Allah and his apostle (Muhammad). How are they to deal with the enemy? By crucifying them, or cutting off their hands and feet on alternate sides, or banishing them from the country.

Generally speaking, Muslim *jihad* is no longer waged by the sword (although isolated incidents such as the assassination of President Anwar Sadat of Egypt fit that description), but the imperative to subjugate non-Muslims remains an essential ingredient of Islamic philosophy, justifying and even demanding the use of any extremity of power to accomplish that purpose.

Only the outer form of *jihad* has changed, not the inner reality. Today, economic *jihad* is the major strategy of Islamic states. What can stand in the way of the tremendous growth of Arab oil wealth and the power it is capable of wielding?

4

Contrasts between Christian and Islamic Theology

"There is no god but God, and Muhammad is the Messenger of God." This confession of faith, a brief eight words in Arabic, sums up the central belief of the world's Muslims. It also establishes the common ground between Islam and other religions that proclaim the existence of a sovereign God who makes Himself known to humankind. Like Judaism and Christianity, the older religions that preceded and influenced it, Islam is both a monotheistic and a revealed religion (in other words, one its followers believe came to man by direct revelation from God).

Although the Islamic conception of God appears similar in some respects to the Judeo-Christian concept, it is also different in several important ways. Having seen in overview how Islam came into being, we now will look at some of those differences between Islam and Christianity. As we deal with the Muslim world, we need to know some of the fundamental principles of their superficially-similar-but-actually-very-different religion. Knowing them—and how they vary from biblical doctrine—we can better understand what motivates the Muslim in his quest to wage and win an ongoing holy war.

Monotheism was the conviction of the prophet Muhammad, and belief in one God is the central pivot around which Islamic doctrine revolves. The Qur'an does not attempt to prove or argue the existence of Allah; it proclaims his existence as a matter of fact. The word *Islam* itself means "submission to God"—nothing less than the total surrender of man's life to the all-knowing, all-powerful Allah.

Furthermore, Muslims believe God has spoken to man through the prophets, particularly the prophet Muhammad who Muslims regard as the final prophet of God. Although Islam acknowledges other prophets before Muhammad's time—the great figures of the Old and New Testaments such as Abraham, Moses, David, and Jesus—Muslims believe God gave Muhammad the complete revelation of the final divine truth. Thus, ultimate knowledge of God can be found only through the pages of the Qur'an. There in the collection of Muhammad's proclamations, which his followers memorized and recorded, Allah allegedly made known his laws and spelled out what he expects from man morally, ethically, and religiously.

Muslim sacred scripture is emphatic that since

Allah has made his will clearly known in the Qur'an, man has no alternative but to obey it literally. The same enormous zeal with which the Qur'an bears witness to God is evident today in the lives and actions of those Muslims who believe that Islam has lost its original fervor because of its compromise with Western godlessness. Man's objective in life, according to Muslim teaching, should be a true knowledge of Allah's word as revealed in the Qur'an, and a total submission to his will. The enforcement of what is perceived to be God's law on earth is of paramount importance to zealous Muslims, as demonstrated in the fanatical pursuit of this goal in Egypt, Pakistan, Syria, and Iran. The assassins of President Sadat declared they had upheld Islam's teachings by killing a man whom they thought to be compromising the Islamic religion. And the Ayatollah Khomeini did not spare the lives of some of his closest friends when they disagreed with his convictions about what form an Islamic government should take in order to satisfy Qur'anic demands.

The phenomenon of religious persecution raises disturbing questions about the relationship between Islam and its "sister" religions, especially Christianity. Are Muslim fanatics correctly interpreting the directives of the Qur'an when they subjugate non-Muslims? If so, doesn't the Qur'an contradict the Bible? And if that is so, how can they both be revelations of one God? Yet Muslims claim to worship the same God Christians do. Obviously, both religions have traveled a long way down different roads since they met and agreed on monotheism and revelation, pure and simple.

Where Christianity and Islam Differ

As was mentioned earlier, on the surface there seems to be a great deal of resemblance between the Islamic view of God, or Allah, and the God of the Judeo-Christian tradition. The Qur'an gives ninety-nine attributes of God, or "most Beautiful Names," with which Christians would agree; among these is that Allah is the All-Powerful, the Creator, the Merciful, and the Compassionate. However, this appearance of agreement is misleading. It would be a mistake to assume that Muslims and Christians perceive God basically in the same manner just because some of their descriptions of Him are similar. On a deeper level, the differences between Muslim and Christian understandings of God are quite substantial and far-reaching, and the differences between their understanding of how man should relate to God and to his fellow man are even greater.

In the final analysis, the Christian perception of God and response to Him make the crucial difference in the lives of committed Christians. Both Islam and Christianity accept by faith what they assert has been revealed to them by God; yet their claims to divine truth rival each other just as their prescriptions for living do. "By their fruits you will know them," Jesus said in Matthew 7:20, reiterating an age-old truth of human nature: a man's behavior is the most convincing demonstration of his understanding of God; and his concept of God exerts a profound influence on the way he acts.

Take again the phenomenon of religious persecution. Certainly the behavior of many professing Christians indicates they are not immune to self-righteousness, prejudice, hatred, and all the other ills of common humanity. But there is nothing in Christianity that condones, much less endorses, such attitudes and behavior. Quite the contrary, the true Christian constantly strives, with the help of God, to weed out of his dealings with others anything that hinders the growth of love. For the genuine Christian, the self-giving love of God revealed in Jesus Christ is the same love the Christian is called upon to show toward others. Jesus' clear instruction to His followers was, "Love one another as I have loved you" (John 15:12).

Christians always have fallen short of the ideal imitation of Christ, and the history of Christianity is filled with spectacular examples of such failure. The Crusades, the Spanish Inquisition of the Middle Ages, and the vicious extremism of contemporary Northern Ireland are among Christianity's most shameful moments of misguided zeal. But the practitioners of such distortions, the

"Christian" extremists, violate their own professed faith. Although Christianity acknowledges and understands human weakness and the persistent tendency to turn against one's neighbor, it considers acts of religious persecution by its own adherents to be ignorant and evil perversions of the love of Christ.

The same is not true of Islam. Judgmentalism is at the core of the Muslim religion, and nothing within it restrains or counters the human temptation to judge and condemn others. While Christianity, despite mistakes and even atrocities committed in its name, remains essentially a faith of love, forgiveness, and new life, Islam is a religion of law, submission, and punishment. The concept "Judge not, that you be not judged" (Matt. 7:1) is completely foreign to the Muslim mind.

The most striking theological focus of the differences between the two religions is the Christian doctrine of the Incarnation, which Islam flatly rejects. The problem seems to have its source in Muhammad's original misunderstanding of the Christian concept of the Son of God. Christians believe that the Son is none other than God in the flesh, having taken human form.

Muhammad, however, influenced by the polytheistic environment of pre-Islamic Arabia, thought that Christians believe God "married" and produced a son. To Muhammad, very rightly, that would be a pagan belief. Furthermore, Muhammad also mistakenly thought that Christians believe the Trinity consists of Jesus, God, and Mary. Considering the various heresies surrounding the worship of Mary at the time of Muhammad's interest in Christianity, it is not too difficult to imagine how he arrived at the erroneous conclusion that Christians worship more than one God.

Muslims regard Jesus as a prophet of God, and they accept His miracles. But Muslims believe that Christian faith in the divinity of Jesus is polytheism. Consequently, although Christians have special status in Islam as "People of the Book," Muslims believe that the Bible in its present form is corrupt and that only the Qur'an contains the ultimate truth.

Thus, to some extent, Islam arose out of a misunderstanding of Christianity—a crucial misunderstanding in view of the tremendous implications it carries. When Muslims reject the concept of God-become-man, they also reject the kind of relationship between God and man that is the essence of the Christian faith. Put simply, Islam delineates a concept of God that ultimately is irreconcilable with the Christian gospel. Muslims do not believe that God would have an interest in a personal relationship of love and friendship with man, much less that He actually would enter into human history for the purpose of establishing, or rather reestablishing, such a relationship. But Christians affirm that this is precisely the meaning of Jesus' life, death, and resurrection. Jesus said to

His disciples, "No longer do I call you servants . . . but I have called you friends" (John 15:15). The Christian gospel emphasizes God's offer of intimate friendship with man—the possibility of loving communion with God. Islam puts exclusive and legalistic emphasis on the commandments of God.

According to Muslims, divinity and humanity are totally exclusive entities. God really could not have entered into human life, and the relationship with God that the Christian enjoys is impossible. Fellowship with God, which is the religious experience of the Christian, is unimaginable to Muslims. They consider the Christian assertion that man was created in God's own image to be blasphemous.

The careful reader of the Qur'an cannot escape the impression that the essence of Allah is power—power overrides all his other attributes. The Creation itself was an act of Allah's absolute power, an expression of his might as lord reigning over all worlds and kingdoms. God's eternal power is clearly demonstrated in the Creation, as the Qur'an testifies:

> See they not the clouds, how they are created? And the heaven, how it is raised high and the mountains, how they are fixed and the earth, how it is spread out? (88:17–20).

In contrast, man is "servant" to his "master," God. God decrees everything that happens, and man has no real choice but to submit to the divine will. Allah's power, of itself, qualifies him to act as arbitrarily as he pleases. According to the Qur'an, "He leads and misleads whom he will" (74:34).

Furthermore, the Qur'an goes so far as to say that man has little choice in determining the purpose of his life:

> Man does not enter the world or leave it as he desires. He is a creature; and the Creator, who has brought him into existence and bestowed upon him higher and more excellent faculties than upon other animals, has also assigned an object to his existence (15:29).

Some of this may sound similar to the Bible, but in the Qur'an the image of the sovereign God is not tempered by a loving, compassionate side. The Qur'an stresses the concept that by God's design man should devote all his faculties to the practice of religion:

> Therefore stand firm in your devotion to the true faith, which Allah himself has made and for which he has made men (30:30).

The Qur'an relates that God created man from the "crackling clay of black mud" and then breathed into him the breath of life:

> He formed and fashioned the body of Adam from the dry clay and then he breathed into the body

of his own spirit; and man, an embodied soul, came into being (15:28,29).

On the surface, the Qur'an parallels the biblical account of creation. The Qur'an, however, stresses the idea that man is God's viceroy, his substitute on earth. It does not attach particular significance to the story of man's fall from his state of communion with God. There are two reasons for that: Muslims do not believe in man's original communion with God as the purpose for which he was created, and they do not believe in original sin.

The Qur'anic view of the nature of man can be expressed this way: Man was created good; in fact, his nature is superior to the angelic hosts themselves, who were commanded to bow down before him at his creation. But being mortal, man is inconstant when tested with evil. He fell through the temptation of Satan, and he lost paradise, but he is not radically estranged from God. Man is prone to sin, but his basic nature is not sinful.

Christians believe that at the Fall something radical happened to man's nature. Man became totally sinful, alienated from God, and incapable of reconciliation with God through his own efforts. Christians also believe that the whole purpose of man's existence is to live in that relationship of loving union with God, which He originally created, but which sin destroyed. Therefore salvation is necessary, and the redemption Jesus Christ effected is both the restoration and the fulfillment of man's reason for being.

That concept is precisely what Muslims deny. Muslims do not see man as totally sinful and incapable of saving himself. Muslims also see a totally different relationship between man and God and, accordingly, cannot understand that man was created in God's image, or that God became man.

Sin and Sinfulness

Much of what the Qur'an says about the practice of sin sounds, again, very much like the Bible. For example, the Qur'an has several words for sin, but behind all of them is the idea of failure to come up to the standards set by God. Man was created for the service of Allah, and he is supposed to obey what he has commanded. The root of sin lies in prideful opposition to God's will. Man is prone to wrong actions due to his weakness; therefore, the only way he can avoid evil is by doing good works according to God's commands. The Qur'an teaches that "Surely good deeds take away evil deeds" (11:114).

But the Qur'an does not consider sin to have tainted the nature of man, and thus Islam has no overall doctrine of sin. The Qur'an reveals that Muhammad himself had no deep conviction concerning sin, and he did not demand that believers experience any such conviction. Rather,

Islam puts forth ideas about specific wrongdoings in order to classify them as great or small for determining the degree of punishment.

Kabira ("great sins") include such things as committing murder or adultery, disobeying God or one's parents, drinking to excess, practicing usury, neglecting Friday prayers and the feast of Ramadan, forgetting the Qur'an after reading it, swearing falsely or by any other name than that of God, performing magic, gambling, dancing, or shaving the beard. Such sins can only be forgiven after repentance. *Saghira* ("little sins") include lying, deception, anger, and lust. Sins of this class are easily forgiven if the greater sins are avoided and if some good actions are performed.

The sin that surpasses all others is *shirk*, the association of other deities with Allah. That is unpardonable. Tradition has it that when Muhammad was asked to identify the greatest sin, he said it was polytheism, the worship of more than one deity. (This, incidentally, is all the justification Muslims would need to wage a holy war on non-Muslims—to convert, conquer, or kill them as unbelievers who have corrupted the true faith.)

The Muslim's view of God is that of an elderly, cherubic Arab who is always happy when people obey him and furiously angry when they disobey—and he rewards or punishes them accordingly. To the faithful, he is Lord of Bounty, but like a benevolent dictator, he insists on compliance with his laws.

Yet Muslims believe Allah can be merciful if he so chooses. He accepts repentance and forgives man's faults and shortcomings. The opening words of each chapter of the Qur'an read, "In the name of God, the merciful." Muslims believe that every word and every accent in the Qur'an reveal the mercies of God.

The Qur'an teaches that forgiveness has to be sought because God is all-knowing (another superficial similarity with the Bible). He sees the secrets of our lives; nothing we do escapes his notice. Allah's *magfera* ("forgiveness") preserves a person from being touched by punishment. That Allah forgives the sins of man is repeatedly proclaimed in the Qur'an, but it is important to remember that forgiveness is purely the prerogative of Allah. There is no atoning blood of Christ to cover the sins of the believer once and for all. Even though he is addressed as "merciful," Allah remains a stern, unbending God.

The Five Pillars

The five pillars of Islam summarize the Muslim's fundamental religious duties and beliefs: (1) reciting the *shahada* ("profession of faith"); (2) praying five times daily; (3) paying the *zakat* ("alms-tax"); (4) fasting and praying during the month of Ramadan; and (5) making the pilgrimage to Mecca at least once in a lifetime if financially able. These are the minimal obligations that every good

Muslim must observe. They alone are not adequate to ensure that one is living a virtuous life, but they are the prerequisites of virtue.

So we see that the major emphasis in Islam is on the acts a believer performs rather than on the attitude of the believer's heart. One gains God's favor by what one does; one is not loved by God simply for who one is.

This emphasis on salvation by works rather than by faith produces anxiety for thoughtful Muslims. It is never possible to be assured that one's actions have earned an acquittal before the eternal Judge of all mankind. The Muslim must be vigilant constantly, exercising an alertness mixed with fear.

The insecurity and fear that are integral to Islam make it both a defensive and an aggressive religion. Just as sin is not essential to the nature of man in the Muslim view, neither is forgiveness essential to the nature of Allah. Allah is not bound by his own nature to forgive man. It is something he chooses to do somewhat consistently, but there is no guarantee that he will do so in every instance. There is no doubt about what Allah expects man to do in this life if he is to have any hope of being admitted to paradise in the next. Nevertheless, no Muslim, no matter how devout and pious, can be sure of winning his favor. Muslims pray to a God they must cajole and beg for forgiveness, and they must bow before a God unwilling to give any assurance that the sinner is forgiven. In a sense, Allah is not entirely trustworthy.

Love and Weakness

The concept of love as one of God's attributes is conspicuously missing in Islam because in Islamic thought love is a sign of weakness. Far be it from Allah, the All-powerful, to be weak. To love is to be vulnerable, and far be it from Allah to be vulnerable. But love also produces genuine confidence and hope and teaches the beloved to love freely and generously in return. Islam has no concept of the strength of love or of the characteristic qualities of love as desirable. The Qur'an gives them no knowledge of the perfect love of God in Jesus Christ, which casts out fear, and which is strong enough to overcome death and inaugurate eternal life here and now. They cannot rest in the promise of a faithful God who assures the Christian that nothing will separate him from the love of God in Jesus Christ.

Whereas in Islam God and man are wary of each other, in Christianity God and man are in love with each other. This difference is of great importance because it lies at the heart of the tensions Muslims feel toward Christians. The same relationship that exists between God and man in each of the two religions exists by extension between man and his fellow man. Christians are taught to love their neighbors as they have first experienced Christ's love. Muslims are taught—many exhortations to charity notwithstanding—to judge, condemn, and even exterminate their neighbors if they fail to measure up to a certain standard of faith and practice, because that is how they expect Allah to deal with them.

Static Theology

Islamic theology is a static theology. Since truth is contained only in a closed book and not primarily in a living, divine Person, they look forward to no further revelation of God, nor to any deepening of their understanding of His nature. They do not think in terms of a process of growth in any area of life. Everything is black and white, cut and dried. Truth is more a proposition to be accepted or rejected than the mystery of God's personal involvement with His creation. The reason Muslims do not understand the Christian gospel is that they have no concept of the spiritual in the Christian sense. Not only do Muslims deny the Second Person of the Trinity (Jesus Christ), but they deny the Third Person (the Holy Spirit) as well. The Holy Spirit, who continuously leads Christians onward into the full awareness of truth, makes no sense at all to Muslims.

In light of Islam's doctrine of salvation by works, the meaning of faith is stunted and crippled. In the absence of a comprehensive doctrine of sin, atonement, or reconciliation with God, has no meaning. Islam, like all expressions of man's religious yearnings, longs for an end to the dominance of sin and death. But because Islam has not fully grasped the tragedy of the situation, it cannot fully appreciate the joy of the solution. Until we experience the Fall, we cannot experience the redemption.

Islam and the Cross

The concept of the cross of Jesus Christ eludes Muslims because they do not understand the need for it. Islam cannot acknowledge the truth of the cross because it cannot see it in the first place. The blinders created by Islam's prejudices about God and man prevent Muslims from looking for the cross or anything like it. Furthermore, substitutionary atonement is to the Muslim mind a primitive and savage idea. Muslims cannot comprehend what to Christians is the highest kind of love—a love that takes the consequences of sin upon itself and finds its meaning in forgiveness.

And yet the cross is present in Islam, too, even if unrecognized. It is ironic, and an affirmation of the mysterious workings of God's grace, that Muslims are required by the Qur'an to read the *Injil*, or Christian gospel, for the value of its moral teaching, even though they reject its most basic message. All Christians should pray sincerely that Muslims genuinely will be instructed by the truth hidden deep within the mandate of their own religion, waiting for them to discover its divine riches. For Christ was speaking to all people when He said, "You shall know the truth, and the truth shall make you free" (John 8:32).

The Day of Judgment

The reality and importance of the Day of Judgment in Islam is second only to the reality and importance of Allah himself. The Qur'an employs some of its most striking language to describe "the event which will overwhelm mankind," when the earth and human society will be destroyed, the dead will be resurrected, and every soul will stand before God to be judged and assigned to dwell for eternity in heaven or hell.

> We moulded man into a most noble image and in the end We shall reduce him to the lowest of the low, except the believers who do good works, for theirs shall be a boundless recompense. What, then can after this make you deny the Last Judgment? Is Allah not the best of judges? (95:4–8).

The God of Islam is not only the benevolent Creator who generously lavishes on mankind all earthly blessings, but also the vengeful Judge who, having demanded submission to his divine will, mercilessly imposes inevitable and terrible punishment on those who spurn him and transgress his laws (in contrast to Christianity's loving God, who, even as He judges in righteousness, is "not willing that any should perish" [2 Pet. 3:9]).

To be a Muslim is to believe in God, the prophecy of Muhammad, and the Last Judgment. But because Islam is a blend in equal proportions of spiritual beliefs and concrete rules of conduct, to be a Muslim is also to live in a specifically prescribed way. Not to do so practically guarantees damnation to unending torment. Thus, in Islam the underlying motivation for faith is fear.

The Qur'an further teaches that man's hour of death is ordained:

> When their doom comes, they are not able to delay it an hour, nor can they advance it (16:61).

Muslims believe that Allah decrees everything that happens, including man's entrance into life and his departure from it. Birth introduces man into this world, and death ushers him into the next. Birth and death are merely two aspects of the phenomenon of life that Allah owns and controls.

The irrevocable finality of death is also very clearly spelled out in the Qur'an. When someone begs Allah to return him to earth, the answer comes:

> By no means! It is but a word that he speaks and before them is a barrier, until the day they are raised (23:100).

Only Allah knows exactly when the Last Judgment will come.

They ask then about the hour when will it come to pass? Say: The knowledge thereof is with my Lord only (7:187).

But there is no doubt in the Qur'an concerning the reality of the day of judgment. It is expected of a Muslim to believe in that reality, almost in the same way as he believes in God. Again, this teaching is much like Christian thought on the subject.

In Islam, the hereafter is divided into heaven and hell. In heaven, believers will experience God's favor and benevolence. In hell, unbelievers will experience God's severity and wrath.

The Qur'an describes both places in vivid terms. Heaven is an oasis-paradise filled with "gardens watered by running streams," rivers of milk, wine, clarified honey, and shade trees bearing all kinds of fruits.

In hell, on the other hand, people will be made to drink boiling water, molten metal, and decaying filth. "Then as for those who are unhappy, they will be in the fire; for them there will be sighing and groaning" (11:106). Hell has seven divisions, each with its particular purpose and terrors for various heretics and unbelievers. There is a Muslim purgatory, a special division of hell for Christians, one for Jews, and a bottomless pit for hypocrites. Obviously, many of these details are at odds with biblical teaching.

As for the Last Judgment itself, the clearest and

most concise description of the Muslim's view is found in L. Bevan Jones's book, *The People of the Mosque*.[1] He divided the events of the Last Day into what he called "the four outstanding features."

According to Muslim tradition, the Last Day will not come until there is no one found who calls on God. Then "the sounding of the trumpet" will signal the arrival of the Day of Judgment. At the first blast of the trumpet, everyone in heaven and earth will die except those whom God saves. At the second trumpet blast, the dead will be resurrected.

After the resurrection, there will follow a period of forty years when people will wander about the earth naked, confused, and sorrowful. They must await "the descent of the books," which have been kept by the recording angels. Each book will be given to its owner, delivered into the right hand of those who are good, and into the left hand of those who are wicked.

Next "the scales" will weigh each one's good and bad deeds, and their fate will be determined. The good deeds are heavy; the bad deeds are light. Prophets and angels will be exempt from this trial, and according to some authorities, so will believers.

Finally, when the preceding tests have been

---

[1]L. Bevan Jones, *The People of the Mosque* (Calcutta: Associated Press, YMCA, 1932).

concluded, everyone will have to cross "the bridge," a very narrow road "sharper than the edge of a sword, finer than a hair, suspended over hell" (36:66). Those who are to be saved will pass over it quickly, but those who are condemned will fall into hell and remain there forever.

Jesus and the Muslim's Day of Judgment

As for knowing when the Last Day is approaching, one of the most popular beliefs among Muslims is that Jesus will return and declare Himself a Muslim, and will call the world to Islam. Then, He will die a normal death. For Muslims believe that when the Roman soldiers came to Jesus at night, before they laid hands on Him, God pulled Him up to heaven. The return of Jesus is one of the definitive signs of the Last Day, in Muslim thinking, presumably because of their belief that Jesus did not die, but was lifted up to heaven before the Crucifixion. It is not difficult to see that Islam has adopted only partial segments of the teaching of the New Testament.

The harshness of Islam is the direct result of its uncertainty about salvation and eternity. Not only are people what they worship, but they become what they fear. The Muslim's fear of Allah's judgment and condemnation turns outward into the same kind of action toward others. Grace and forgiveness are rare attributes of God or man in

80

Islam, which proves a common saying that "Islam is as arid as the deserts of its birth."

Islam has failed to perceive accurately God's declared purpose for man, or why God is interested in man at all. Muslims bend over backwards paying homage to the power of God out of the erroneous belief that God is mainly concerned with exacting tribute from man. In this regard Islam is curiously like the pre-Islamic tribal religions it so strenuously rejected. Christians believe that one reason Christ's coming was necessary was that, at the time of Jesus, Judaism had become such a distortedly legalistic religion. The Jews did not understand that God was much more interested in the inward attitude of the believer's heart than in his outward show of religion. Islam is similar to Judaism in that respect.

The tragedy of Islam is that, because it does not recognize God's real concern for reestablishing a relationship of love with mankind, Muslims deprive themselves of the joy of participating in that relationship. Paradoxically, in the effort to accord Allah all the honor his power deserves, Islam has seriously underestimated the real power of God. Muslims simply are unable to comprehend the tremendous power of divine love that chose to live humbly as a man among men in order that all might know God.

5

Sunni—Shi'ite Division

Americans seem blissfully unaware of the threat to their oil supply and their total physical well-being that is posed by the strong probability that the shah's regime in Iran will not be the last Middle East government to fall to Islamic extremists.

In October 1981, Iranian pilgrims bound for Mecca were deported by Saudi troops for carrying Khomeini's posters and tracts calling for the overthrow of the Saudi regime. In December of the same year, another event shocked the Middle East. A group of Shi'ite Muslims from several Arab states sought unsuccessfully to overthrow Bahrain's Sunni government.

The current instability in the governments of the Middle East grows out of several long-standing disputes in the Arab Muslim world over such issues as fundamentalism versus secularism, politics versus religion, and the Sunni branch of Islam versus the Shi'ite branch. In this chapter I will concentrate on the last of these conflicts and the threat it poses to the West's economic and other interests.

The Iran-Iraq war is widening the old divisions within Islam. The fanatical Ayatollah Ruhollah Khomeini in Iran is trying to increase the importance of his Shi'ite sect of Islam at the expense of all the others. Perhaps a way to explain the differences between the sects in Islam would be to compare them to the different denominations of Christianity. During the Protestant Reformation, there was a split in the Christian church, and Protestants left the dominant branch of Christianity, the Roman Catholic church. Following the Reformation, the Protestants split into several branches. Something similar happened in Islam. After the death of Ali, the fourth caliph (successor to Muhammad), Islam split into two groups. The splinter group (the followers of Ali) then split again. Khomeini is the leader of one of these splinter sects, Twelver Shi'ite Islam.

A Brief History of Shi'ism

Following the death of Muhammad, his trusted friend Abu Bakr was named the first caliph. Abu Bakr was one of the first converts to Islam, Muhammad's close advisor, and also his father-in-law. The choice of Abu Bakr to lead the newly founded Islamic *Ummah* ("community of believers") disappointed Ali (Muhammad's cousin, son-in-law, and close friend). Ali felt that he was Muhammad's legitimate heir and therefore should have been named caliph. Only after two more successors, Umar and Othman, had died in power did Ali become caliph. Following his ascension, a power struggle ensued, and Ali was assassinated by Mu'awiya (founder of the Umayyad Dynasty). The caliphate passed on to the monarchical House of Umayyad. However, Ali's son, Hussein, claimed that as Muhammad's grandson, the caliphate belonged to him. The struggle that followed split the Muslim world into supporters of the House of Ali and supporters of the House of Umayyad. Hussein was killed in a battle with Caliph Yazid of the Umayyads. The split became permanent with his death, the two main groups being the *Shi-at Ali* (the party of Ali), supporting the descendants of Ali as rightful rulers, and the Sunni (the followers of the Prophet's Path), supporting first the Umayyads and then the Abbasids.

Defeated by the Sunnis, the Shi'ites felt a deep sense of having been wronged:

> They became dissenters, subversives within the Arab empire, given to violence against authority. Shiite Islam was an extremely emotional sect and still is. Its adherents at times clothe themselves in black cloaks and black turbans, and once a year reenact the passion of Husayn [Hussein], sometimes flagellating themselves as a means of atoning for Husayn's [Hussein's] martyrdom.[1]

---

[1]James Cook, "Sunnis? Shiites? What's that got to do with oil prices?", *Forbes* (April 12, 1982), p. 99.

Shi'ites insist that the descendants of Ali are the *Imams* ("leaders"). Imams are considered to be sinless, almost infallible leaders in all spheres of life, including politics. They also are able to interpret and reinterpret the Qur'an. Shi'ites believe in a continuing revelation of God's word through the Imams.

The Twelver Shi'ite sect of Khomeini teaches that the infant Twelfth Imam went into hiding in the ninth century and will remain hidden until the end of time, when he will return to earth as the *Mahdi* ("Messiah") in order to establish the millennium of perfect equity.

Twelver Shi'ites believe that until the Twelfth Imam returns, every true Muslim must put himself under the authority of a holy man—an ayatollah. This belief has given rise to a strong clergy and a religious hierarchy. From those men alone can salvation come. They also wield enormous secular power.

Early in the sixteenth century, Twelver Shi'ism was made the official religion of Persia (now called Iran). The clergy became increasingly powerful. In other Muslim countries, Sunni religious authorities were absorbed into the state; they became part of the civil service in Egypt. The Shi'ite clergy, on the other hand, developed a tradition of opposition to the state. They believed that the state owed religious obedience to them. In 1906 the Shi'ite clergy in Persia led the revolution that established a constitution and caused the fall of the two-hundred-year-old Qajar dynasty. They caused the rise of the first Pahlavi Shah, Reza Shah, and the fall of the second, Muhammad Shah.

Khomeini and His Influence

Playing on the Twelver Shi'ites' expectation of the return of the Twelfth Imam, Khomeini claimed to be a linear descendant of Ali and took for himself the title of Imam. He was thus able to stir up the emotions of the people and broaden his power base. Ayatollah Khomeini was successful in deposing the shah and re-creating Iran so that it would conform to his ideology. He has built a state in which the clergy has absolute control; there is no secular authority with which to contend.

Not content with changing Iran, Khomeini is attempting to export his concept of religious government. Khomeini propaganda calling for the downfall of Saddam Hussein in Iraq precipitated the current border war. However, the Shi'ite majority in Iraq do not seem prepared for Khomeini's style of government; they have not withdrawn support from Hussein. The war is taking its toll in both countries. The Iranian and Iraqi economies are in shambles as a result of financing a long war. Iran is sending every able-bodied male into battle. At the Ramadi prisoner of war (POW) camp about sixty-five miles west of Baghdad, Iraq, prisoners range in age from thirteen-year-olds to white-haired, old men. The youngest of the prisoners seemed on the verge of tears as he described how he had been given three months of training before being sent to the front near Khorramshahr. They were told the Iraqis were all heathens, and it was their holy duty to fight them.

To stir up the Shi'ites residing in Iraq, Khomeini declared that Saddam Hussein is Mu'awiya (the original antagonist of Ali fourteen hundred years ago) coming back from the grave to kill him. What Khomeini subtly communicated was that he is Ali—the Prophet's true successor.

Today there is a well-organized network throughout the Arab world of Khomeini-type radicals who promote Khomeini's ideas by selling his Arabic tapes in almost every capital city in the Middle East.

In writing the book *The Missing Religious Duty*, engineer Muhammad Abdel Salam Farag, one of the five accused assassins of Anwar Sadat, was influenced greatly by Khomeini's ideas.

The Danger for the Future

As Iran's Ayatollah Khomeini continues to export his brand of Islamic government, the very real possibility is that more-moderate Sunni governments around the Persian Gulf will be overthrown by radical Shi'ites (or, at the very least, Sunni governments will become more radical in an effort to appease their Shi'ite populations). As noted earlier, a coup has already been attempted in Bahrain, and rulers in such nations as Saudi Arabia and Kuwait also have reason for worry.

We have described basic Islamic ideology as anti-Western and anti-Christian regardless of the different branches of Islam. The religion as a whole is dedicated to world domination. But it is also true that some Muslims are more ideologically oriented than others—that some, like Shi'ites responsive to the teachings of Khomeini, are more passionately opposed than others to the West and everything about it. If such people take control of more of the oil-rich nations in the Middle East— again, a real possibility—the status of our vital oil supplies from those states immediately would be far less secure. It is almost certain that the wealth of those nations would be used to promote Islamic superiority even more aggressively than at present.

6

Egypt, Case of a Conquered Nation

Egypt is a poignant case study of the way Islam can drown a nation. It serves as an example of what happens when Islamic revolutionaries call for revival. The power struggle between radical Muslims and the moderate leadership of any modern Muslim state is inevitable; the two forces cannot peacefully coexist. Egypt's moderate leaders have tried continually to align themselves with the West—not only to loosen the Russian tentacles on their land and economy, but also to erect a solid dyke against militant revolutionaries with their threat to political stability. The West, for its part, has poured its hopes for the Middle East into Egypt, counting on its pro-Western leadership to give impetus and direction for a comprehensive peace settlement.

Since President Anwar Sadat's assassination, however, disconcerting questions have arisen: How well-founded is that hope for peace now? Was a man or an idea killed? Was Sadat's assassination an isolated incident without implications? Or was it part of the same pattern of anti-modernistic, anti-Western Islamic resurgence that swept Iran?

President Hosni Mubarak, Sadat's hand-picked successor, vows "no change" in government policies established by Sadat. But can he continue to steer a moderate course in the midst of the tensions and conflicts that are mounting in Egyptian society? Sadat was hated both inside and outside his country by Islamic fundamentalists, who are increasing in numbers as well as fervor.

Peace Mission and Death Warrant

When Anwar Sadat traveled to Jerusalem in November 1977 on his mission for peace in the Middle East, he stirred the fury of the Islamic world against him. In the eyes of the West, Sadat's peace initiative was an act of vision, courage, and statesmanship of the highest order. To great numbers of Muslims, however, Sadat had committed high treason. They interpreted the independent gesture by which he sought an end to the continual hatred, war, and violence of the Arab-Israeli blood-feud as a betrayal. Not only did he break the twenty-nine-year-old Arab ban on direct dealings with the Israelis, which had existed since the founding of the State of Israel in 1948, but his declared willingness, proclaimed to Israel's Knesset, "to live with you in permanent peace and justice," amounted to heresy in the minds of many of his fellow Muslims.

Until Sadat's pilgrimage, no leader on either side had taken such a radical step forward on the road to peace. His bold trip to Jerusalem and the negotiations that followed became the means for breaking the political deadlock of the preceding three decades.

The peace process he inaugurated bore its first fruit at Camp David, Maryland, where Sadat, Israeli Prime Minister Menachem Begin, and United States President Jimmy Carter sequestered themselves for thirteen days in September 1978 and hammered out the historic "framework for peace." More lengthy and precarious negotiations followed while the rest of the world watched and waited. Finally, on March 26, 1979, at an emotional White House ceremony, the three leaders signed a formal treaty. For the first time in thirty-one years, Egypt and Israel were no longer in a state of war.

However, it was a costly irony. When Sadat signed the peace treaty, he also, in effect, signed his own death warrant. The Islamic world wanted him dead. Peace-loving people of all nationalities were stunned and grief-stricken when President Sadat was assassinated on October 6, 1981, by a band of Muslim fanatics. But while some mourned his loss and paid him tribute, great throngs in many Islamic countries took to the streets, rejoicing in the "death of the infidel." "Sadat was doomed from the day he went to Jerusalem," declared Lieutenant General Saadeddin Shazli, one of Egypt's most famous political exiles. "Anyone who follows in that traitorous path will similarly be doomed."

His assassins were extremists, but their action was not really surprising. It was a deliberate attempt to purify Islam, to eliminate what they considered a corrupt element.

What We Need to Understand

There is a strain of Western liberal thinking, idealistic rather than pragmatic, that asks simplistic questions such as the following: What is wrong with an attempt to square political conduct with religious principles? Isn't it understandable, even laudable, for leaders to try to remodel public and private life? This attitude assumes there is no reason why the West's encounters with militant Islam ultimately should be unpleasant because, after all, Islam is monotheistic and one of the world's higher religions. What this naive and unrealistic approach ignores is the philosophy of Islamic literalism which makes militant Islam both powerful and dangerous, as I have illustrated throughout this book.

Islamic philosophy divides the world into two camps—believers and infidels. Infidels are to be humiliated, to be denied the due process of law, and ultimately, to be converted or killed. Islam's simple vindication of this is found in the Qur'an:

> Fight against such of those who have been given the Scripture as believe not in Allah nor the Last Day . . . (9:29).

No genuine Christian reformer could pursue such a philosophy and remain true to Christian doctrine. But to follow such a strategy is precisely what makes a Muslim true to Islam. Using this same scripture as justification, Muslim zealots consider moderate Muslims, who do not follow the letter of the law, to be infidels also, equally deserving the same treatment.

By its philosophy and style, the Muslim Brotherhood of Egypt is an example of the type of radical movements that exist in virtually every Islamic state. They are religious organizations bent on applying Islamic law literally. Founder of the Egyptian Muslim Brotherhood, Hasan Al-Banna, forcefully expressed the viewpoint of those groups to his followers:

> You are not a benevolent organization, nor a political party, nor a local association with limited aims. Rather, you are a new spirit making its way into the heart of this nation, and reviving it through the Qur'an; a new light dawning and scattering the darkness of materialism through

the knowledge of God; a resounding voice rising
and echoing the message of the Apostle.[1]

The extreme sense of religious superiority these
groups exhibit has created problems within Islam
itself. Shukri Ahmed Mustafa, a leader of the
Muslim Brotherhood offshoot group accused in
the killing of the former Egyptian minister of
Trusts and Bequests, said his movement's philosophy was based on "sacred hatred" of Islamic
nations he believes have departed from the true
faith. "Spilling the blood of heretics is the sacred
duty of all Muslims," Mustafa told a reporter
before he was hanged in 1978. Indeed, the
assassination of President Sadat was part of an old
pattern of attempts to prod the masses into Islamic
revolution, which would lead to the "Islamic
Republic of Egypt."

The Muslim Brotherhood of Egypt did not come
to the world's attention until Sadat was killed, but
it existed long before the tragic event that cata-
pulted it to notoriety. While the Brotherhood is far
from a majority movement in Egypt, it exerts
much influence. Since its founding in 1928, it has
been dedicated to establishing a modern political
community based upon a return to the fundamental precepts of Islam. In the 1950s, the Brotherhood

---

[1]Hasan Al-Banna, "Between Yesterday and Today," *Five
Tracts of Hasan Al-Banna*, trans. Charles Wendell (Berkeley:
University of California Press, 1978), p. 36.

rapidly gained such power that President Gamal Abdel Nasser imprisoned its leaders, and many members of the group were placed in concentration camps or hanged because of assassination attempts on Nasser. Imprisonment and hard labor continued for the Brotherhood until President Sadat came to power in 1970. Ironically, Sadat released the Muslim Brotherhood's leaders from prison in an effort to impress the democratic West.

To the Islamic purist, such as a Brotherhood member, all other religions are either heretical or hopelessly corrupt. He tolerates no other view; he also believes that it is Allah's will for all societies to come under the Islamic flag and for Islamic law and religion to control and undergird all of life for all people. In other words, only a doctrinally pure, incorrupt Islamic nation can please Allah. Anything else must be redeemed or destroyed.

Islam Invades Egypt

A glance at Egypt's history will illustrate the way Islam can invade, permeate, and subvert a nation and culture. Although over the centuries Islam ultimately became the majority religion in Egypt, that national religious conversion was not accomplished without much bloodshed and destruction.

For twenty-five centuries, Egypt was occupied by every rising power in the known world, from the Assyrians and the Hellenist Greeks to the Romans and Byzantines. Then, before Egypt was

97

able to take a single breath of freedom, the Muslims came roaring in from their sandy tribal ghettos. Those latter invaders not only occupied Egypt as had the previous powers, but through their cultural imperialism they permeated every area of Egyptian life, becoming an integral part of it within a few years.

Egypt's original heritage was seen only dimly in the lives of a minority of Christians who refused total submission to the Arab conquerors. The high cost of refusal was often their own deaths. Through manipulation, blackmail, and outright obliteration of resistance, Islam became the religion of the majority in Egypt. Few people were able to pay the high taxes the Muslims imposed, so their only alternative (if they wanted to live) was to accept Islam, to become "part of the faithful." Those too poor to pay taxes, yet unwilling to convert to Islam, were martyred.

The largest group to withstand the onslaught of Islam was the Coptic church in Egypt. Founded in A.D. 42 by Mark, the author of the second Gospel, the Coptic church had six hundred years to become established before the Muslims overran Egypt. The Copts have retained much of their original heritage, and with seven million members, they make up 20 percent of the Egyptian population.

Life has not ceased to be difficult for the Copts in modern times. Radical Islamic organizations persecute, while the government attempts to return to the concept of the *dhimmi*, thereby making Copts second-class citizens.

The Muslim Brotherhood and other radical Muslim groups have made Egyptian Copts a special target for their violence. Property is destroyed; people are beaten, maimed, and killed. For example, on August 14, 1977, Muslims destroyed Christian shops, restaurants, homes, the cathedral, and a Protestant church in Assyuit. Then, during Lent 1978, following a Lenten service a priest, Father Tadros Darwood, was stabbed by Muslim extremists. At the same time, radical Muslims attacked the Fakhoury Monastery; a deacon was killed and a priest injured.

The violence has not abated in recent years. Christians are being told to renounce their faith. In the district of Samulat, on September 3, 1978, the Muslim Brotherhood attacked the Reverend Gabriel Abd-El-Mutgali and his wife. Mutgali was killed after the fanatics had gouged out his eyes with red-hot irons, and they left his wife permanently crippled.

In Menshat, radical Muslims executed two men. Dr. Emad Hanna and Boushra Barbary were beheaded because they attempted to build a church in their own village.

The violence extends to historic monuments. In Cairo, on March 21, 1979, the Church of the Virgin Mary was destroyed. That church was mentioned in a history that was written in A.D. 864. The eleven-hundred-year-old structure was completely gutted when a Muslim extremist exploded a napalm bomb inside.

Egyptian Law

In each of those cases, little or no action was taken by Egyptian authorities. The police do not extend equal protection to all citizens. Following an incident of arson at a church in Abou Teig in Upper Egypt, the police closed the church. They then requested that the priest sign a declaration stating that he would not conduct prayers in the church. When he refused, he was told that the police were not responsible for his safety. The church was attacked again, and one young Christian burned to death in the resulting fire. The police did nothing.

In the town of Basatten, near Cairo, a church was seized by a radical Muslim organization. The Muslims converted it into a mosque. When the Christians complained to the authorities that their property had been taken, the police demolished the building because the Christians had not had the proper permits for construction of the church.

Egyptian law states that no church may be built or have any alterations, repairs, or improvements without a presidential decree. That law was enacted in 1856, following the outline of the "Covenant of Umar." (The statute was placed on the books by the Ottoman Empire when Egypt was one of its colonies.) In 1972, President Anwar

Sadat promised Coptic leaders that he would give fifty permits per year for church building. During the period between 1973 and 1979, he gave a total of fifty permits. In 1978 and in 1979, he gave five permits.

By 1980, there were one hundred outstanding applications for permits, which had been accumulating for years. Christian churches sometimes wait as long as twenty-seven years for a permit to build, while the government builds mosques almost daily and pays mosque leaders. Since taking office, President Mubarak has reactivated and tightened this law, making it literally impossible for new churches to be erected or old churches to be renovated.

Churches that already exist are having their lands taken from them by the government. The police seized the trust land of the Monastery of St. Bishoy on orders from the Ministry of Islamic Affairs. The Christian donor had indicated that the land was to be used for the benefit of the monks and visitors to the monastery. The reason given for the seizure was that a Muslim could visit the monastery, and according to Islamic law, non-Muslims (the monks) should not be guardians for Muslim visitors.

Using the Qur'anic admonition that non-Muslims should have no authority over Muslims, the Ministry of Islamic Affairs seized thousands of acres of land. Those trust lands had been under the jurisdiction of Christian churches and charities

101

for as long as one hundred years. In one case, after the seizure was contested, the Ministry offered restitution of 35,000 Egyptian pounds for lands valued at 5 million pounds.

Governmental prejudice in Egypt extends to the courts. Mr. Abdel Hamed Soliman, a Supreme Court judge, wrote an article about justice in the January 1979 edition of *Al-Daowa* magazine. In it he stated that according to Islamic laws, a Christian should not be a judge in a court case in which a Muslim was involved. He cited the decision by the Court of Appeals in Alexandria in 1978, which reversed the decision of a lower court because the judge was a Christian and the defendant was a Muslim.

As mentioned before, Christians are forbidden from testifying in court cases involving Muslims. On May 19, 1970, the Domestic Section of the Supreme Court in Egypt rendered a decision in the following case.

A childless, wealthy Christian woman donated half of her property to a Christian charity organization in Alexandria; the other half she left to her relatives. When she died, she was buried in a chapel built with her own money.

One of her nephews, a Muslim, claimed that his aunt adopted Islam before her death, making him the only beneficiary according to Islamic principles.

There were no official records to confirm his

claim. Egypt requires that all changes in religion be registered.

The nephew brought his aunt's Muslim cook and the cook's husband to support his claim. The Christian charity and the other relatives brought the priests and nuns who took care of the woman during her illness and who were with her when she died. All of the witnesses for the defense were Christians.

The court decided in favor of the nephew because the testimony of "infidels" is not valid against a Muslim. The Muslim nephew was given all of his aunt's property. According to Islamic law, no non-Muslim should inherit property from a Muslim.

The courts set another precedent in a case where they annulled the marriage of a young couple because the girl converted to Christianity from Islam.

Shirin Saleh, in accordance with Egyptian law, notified the Governorate of Alexandria that she wished to become a Christian. On July 2, 1971, she was baptized. Later that month, she married an Orthodox Christian.

The couple was summoned to the police department for investigation. They presented her notice of change of religion and their marriage certificate. (It is illegal for a Muslim woman to marry a non-Muslim.)

Upon the directive of the Ministry of the Interior,

the *Parquet* (the Attorney General) office in Alexandria filed suit No. 224/1972, requesting that the marriage be declared null and void and that the couple be separated.

The case was first heard before the Alexandria Court of Personal Status Matters on June 12, 1972. The court ruled in favor of the *Parquet*. The court declared that, according to Muslim law, anyone who renounces Islam is deserving of the death sentence, and therefore should be considered legally dead; the court stated that dead people cannot be married.

An appeal was filed with the Alexandria Court of appeals on the following grounds: (1) the *Parquet* was not a party of interest, and therefore could not institute the case; (2) because the defendants were both Christians of the same sect, their marriage could not possibly be governed by Muslim law; and (3) Muslim rules regarding *Riddah* (renouncing Islam) are contrary to freedom of religion as safeguarded in the Egyptian constitution.

The court of appeals upheld the lower court in 1974, on the following grounds:

(1) The Egyptian society is a Muslim society, hence ruled by the Muslim law, and the *Parquet* representing the society derives its right of claim in cases of *Riddah* from Muslim law direct.

(2) According to Egyptian Legislation No. 462/1955, and in point of principle, the Muslim law is the common law of the land. A married couple of Christian creed, if of the same sect, would be subject to their own Personal Status law, provided that this would not trespass on the "Public Order" in Egypt. The Muslim rules of *Riddah* are of "Public Order" and therefore should prevail.

(3) As to the appellant's argument regarding the freedom of religion, Section II of the Egyptian constitution was invoked in that it declared Islam to be the Religion of the State, hence freedom of religion should be viewed within this frame.

(4) The reasons of the judgment of the first instance declaring the above-said marriage null and void were right and worthy of confirmation.[2]

Since 1973, Egypt has moved toward making the country totally Islamic. Urged on by radical Islamic organizations, the way is being paved by legislation making the Qur'an the major source of law. Court decisions are setting precedents wherein non-Muslims are being pushed more and more into the role of the *dhimmi*.

---

[2]Extraction from the Judgment of the Court of Appeals in Alexandria on June 9, 1974, sub. no. 25/1972, Personal Status Matters.

In response to governmental refusal to adequately respond to Coptic complaints, Pope Shenouda of the Coptic church canceled all official Easter festivities for 1980. He restricted Easter celebrations to simple prayers. Refusing to accept President Sadat's annual Easter greetings, the pope patriarch and the members of the Holy Synod (the governing body of the church) retired to the desert monastery of St. Bishoy. Angered by the worldwide press attention caused by this and other moves, President Sadat attacked Coptic leaders in a speech on May 14 of that year. He accused them of plotting to overthrow his government, of slandering both him and Egypt, and of attempting to foster social discontent. Sadat then placed the Christian leaders under house arrest at the monastery. He removed the pope and the synod from their positions of authority within the church. In their stead, he appointed a council of bishops, which was to be more responsive to governmental policies.

Following the assassination of Sadat on October 6, 1981, virtually all of his political prisoners were released, including leaders of the Muslim Brotherhood. President Mubarak has yet to release the Coptic leaders, nor has he allowed them to resume their duties as the ruling body of the church.

Only One Example

Egypt is just one illustration of what happens to a nation when Islam takes over. Similar stories could be told about other Muslim states. Typically, only Muslims are regarded as full citizens with all the rights of citizenship. In Saudi Arabia, for example, non-Muslims cannot be citizens at all. Also in Saudi Arabia, no Christian churches of any kind can be built, and those established in other buildings by foreigners for their own benefit cannot be publicly identified as such.

Those policies in Egypt, Saudi Arabia, and other Islamic states are consistent with the Muslim mandate to convert or conquer the world. Since to the Muslim there is only one true religion (Islam) and there are no such things as freedom of religion or separation of church and state, such laws are the natural outgrowth of his faith's demand that he bring all the world under its banner. Just as those policies and practices have been implemented in Egypt, they will be put in effect in any other nation that comes under Muslim domination.

7

Russia and the Foreign Policy Dilemma

The West's confrontation with the current resurgence of Islam has created an enormous foreign policy problem for Western nations attempting to respond intelligently and constructively to the complexities of Middle Eastern affairs. Since 1973, in the aftermath of the Arab–Israeli War and the oil embargo imposed by Muslim countries, the West has been forced to observe something "new" in the Middle East—namely, Western economic dependence on the outcome of events over which it has little control. Western nations can ill afford for the Middle East to explode and for world oil supplies to be cut, but there is little agreement about how to handle relations with Muslim nations.

To compound the threat of Islamic extremism, an added danger is the pragmatic alliances being struck between Islamic states in the Middle East and the Soviet Union, which has worked to gain influence there for the past twenty-five years. Many people like to think such cooperation is not possible between the followers of Allah and the atheistic Soviets. They assume Muslims hate godless communism at least as much as they hate Western capitalism.

The lesson of recent history, however, is that such thinking is only a fond illusion. While not embracing communism, several Islamic states have proved willing to focus on antagonism toward the West, which they share with the Soviets, rather than on what separates them from the Soviets. Of course, each side in such alliances is seeking to use the other for its own ends. But some of the results of Islamic–Soviet cooperation are that South Yemen is virtually a Soviet colony and Russian military installations are in Libya, Syria, and Iraq.

Even Iran's ruling Islamic Republic Party (IRP) has laid aside its scruples. In October 1981, the IRP enlisted the aid of a team of thirty-six Soviet intelligence agents. This was the first of several Russian advisory missions that assisted Khomeini's government in building up intelligence and security forces and gave muscle to the Islamic Guard, the clergy's private army.

The fundamentalist IRP no doubt flinched slightly at the thought of enlisting help from the Soviets. After all, conscientious Muslims should denounce communism and its atheism. But as the party watched its cadres die in bombings and other assassinations, expediency outweighed philosophy. Besides, the Tudeh Communist Party in Iran had persuaded the IRP's leaders that the *Mujahedin*, the group blamed for the violence, were "CIA-backed leftists." One wonders if it occurred to anyone that the Communists themselves might have stirred the violence in the hope that "Big Brother" might be invited in to quell it, as the Soviets claimed they were doing in Afghanistan, or that the Russians craftily could have maneuvered to gain the foothold in Iran they had coveted for decades.

It was not the first time, of course, that Communists had found a welcome in an Islamic state. In fact, Soviet advisors, with a team of East Germans, were in Iran trying to help shore up the revolution-sapped economy. Cuba's Foreign Minister Isidor Malmierca Peoli zipped in and out of Iran eight times between the shah's fall and the arrival of the Russians. In turn, an Iranian delegation visited Havana where they listened to Fidel Castro applaud Khomeini for leading an "anti-imperialist struggle."

Such cooperation between atheistic communism and the most rabid of Islamic nations does not square with the foreign policy assumptions by which Western policymakers have been guided for years. J. B. Kelly was right when he said,

Surely the time is long overdue for a thorough housecleaning of our conventional assumptions about Islam in its relationship to the West, to rid ourselves in particular of those musty and dangerous illusions about an identity of Muslim and Western interests in opposing the Soviet Union, whose persistence is obscuring both the menace which now confronts us in the (Persian) Gulf and the urgent necessity to counteract it.[1]

Meeting Points Between Islam and Communism

The Soviets and many of their Marxist comrades have noted correctly that there is a grand opportunity in stirring up Islamic fervor. The truth is that there are actually meeting points between Islam and communism that sometime make atheism less conspicuous to Muslims.

The *first* meeting point is economics. By the mid-1960s, Socialist ideology had influenced all Muslim countries to some extent, and communism itself had found many supporters in Islamic lands. Muslims are great consumers of slogans, and the Socialist slogans appealed to them. In fact, many of the same expectations for material well-being are aroused by the preaching of militant Muslims as by Communist propaganda. But because of the vast cultural differences between Russian and Islamic societies, and because of the centrality of Islam in Arab culture, individual Muslim leaders have developed their own brands of socialism, as in the cases of Gamal Abdel Nasser

---

[1]J. B. Kelly, "Islam Through the Looking Glass," *The Heritage Lectures* (Washington: The Heritage Foundation, 1980), p. 11.

in Egypt, Mu'ammer Qadhafi in Libya, Saddam Hussein in Iraq, and Hafez Assad in Syria.

Muslims share the Communist concept of a classless society. In pilgrimages to Mecca, for instance, every Muslim worshiper dresses identically. The richest oil baron wears the same simple, white robe as an insignificant, poverty-stricken pilgrim. And as with the Communists, being classless for Muslims is largely a matter of appearance. Muslim princes and Soviet tyrants live more royally than the poor, who simply remain poor.

Muhammad envisioned an economic system tied to the laws of Islam, which he believed would create the just society. But since Islamic law is meant to be the law of the state, that leads to a level of political control matched only in Marxist societies and other dictatorships.

Views conflict sharply on Muhammad's intentions in founding the Islamic *Ummah*. Some see Islam primarily as an economic and sociopolitical movement. Others argue that Muhammad was a religious reformer who found himself, somewhat against his will, ablaze with a divine message with which he, in turn, set his people afire, irrespective of the consequences. Actually, Islam is a combination of sociopolitical, economic, and religious ingredients, stirred into the melting pot of mysticism and fanaticism.

Muhammad's intention, it appears, was to launch both a new religion and a new society.

Muhammad seemed quite satisfied that the Muslims in Arabia would find the Qur'an the only source of guidance for the totality of daily life. Religion, politics, business and commerce, general economics, and sociological questions, including civil law, moral codes of conduct, ethics, and behavior, are all regulated by the Qur'an.

Muhammad had broad aims for the "complete way of life" of Islam. Not only did he send messages to neighboring rulers (Christians, Jews, and others) to persuade them to convert to Islam, but he also wanted to lead an expedition to Syria. He was not content to preach and let people make up their own minds. He was prevented from mounting any military compaigns, however, by the sickness that led to his death, but his intentions were carried out later by Abu Bakr, his immediate successor, and by subsequent Islamic conquerors. Thus, a *second* meeting point between Islam and communism is that both are oriented to expansion through conquest and revolution.

Mao's dictum that political power comes from the barrel of a gun would fit well with the Islamic notion of *jihad* ("holy war"). According to Islamic teaching, permanent peace with nations other than Muslim states is out of the question. *Jihad* must continue until Islam dominates the whole world. Nothing could be closer to communism's avowed intent to take over the world and destroy the West.

The *third* meeting point between Islam and

communism is the fact that both are anti-Western. Their shared animosity toward the West reconciles the Muslim extremist with the Marxist revolutionary. As an old Arab maxim puts it, "The enemy of my enemy is my friend." J. B. Kelly noted that communism and Islam are "directed against the West, which is seen as the source of trouble and oppression, and against 'imperialism,' which is equated with capitalism, the economic basis of Western society."[2]

One of the least surprising dimensions of the Iranian revolution was its bitter anti-Western thrust, especially as the West was identified with the United States. Tyrants retain power only as they redirect the people's attentions away from their own ignominies, thus maintaining focus on an "enemy." Khomeini was able to point to American support for the shah (who was, admittedly, guilty of a great many ignominies of his own). The United States became, in the zealous Islamic mind, the "Great Satan." Similarly, in other Arab states, American support of Israel has been a major reason for their strident anti-Western slant.

A *fourth* meeting point between Islam and communism is the disdain for democracy. In their secret chambers, most Islamic Arab leaders admire the totalitarian form of government and the ability to deliver the goods while, at the same time, they storm the West, making mockery of its

---

[2]Kelly, "Islam Through the Looking Glass," p. 3.

democratic process as slow, ineffective, and irritat-
ing.

In the West we glorify institutions, respect them
and, as far as possible, abide by those guidelines,
while in Islamic nations the people's respect and
loyalty are normally for a charismatic leader rather
than for institutions. In most cases that leads to
totalitarian dictatorship. The founder of Islam was
not only the religious leader and the prophet, he
was also the political and economic leader. Since
that time, it has been difficult for genuine Western-
style democracy to flourish in an Islamic environment.

Soviet Strategy

How have the Soviets been able to achieve this
dramatic synthesis between certain Islamic powers
and communism? They have accomplished it
through a persistent, skilled, and subtle program
of propaganda, infiltration, and subversion. Not
long after the 1917 revolution put them in power,
the Soviet Communists recognized that the Middle East would play a critical role in world affairs.
Lenin foresaw a period when Middle Eastern oil
would be the sea on which Western economies
would set sail. Among the first nations with which
the new Soviet state established diplomatic relations were Iran, Afghanistan, Yemen, and Saudi
Arabia.

Vladimir Sakharov, a former member of an elite

corps of Soviet specialists on the Middle East, has provided critical information on how the Marxist penetration of Islam occurred. The Institute of International Relations in Moscow is the center for developing a diplomatic strike force, which is then dispatched to the Middle East. In the 1960s, Sakharov was among its graduates. Now the number of Soviet "Arabists" totals nearly three thousand. According to Sakharov, those Russians are

> fluent in local languages, conversant with Islamic law, history, customs, and sensibilities, regional economics and politics, and trained in military tactics, intelligence gathering, propaganda techniques, and recruitment.

Sakharov, unhappy with the Soviet system, became an American agent. He remained within the Soviet Middle Eastern apparatus while working for United States intelligence. "I have watched with pain and dismay," said Sakharov,

> as Washington, apparently believing in detente instead of its own intelligence data, has pursued a complacent, confusing, naive, inconsistent, and suicidal Middle Eastern policy while the American public has been kept largely ignorant of the gains the Soviets have continued to make.[3]

[3]Vladimir Sakharov, speech reprinted in *Air California* (December 1980), pp. 46–48.

Russian policy has been to give aid and support to foreign countries, not on the condition that a nation be Marxist, but simply that it be "anti-imperialist" or voice anti-Western sentiment. Muslim states, such as Syria, Libya, Iraq, and South Yemen, maintain similar policies. Sakharov explains that the Soviet government deploys Russian Muslims in key diplomatic posts in all Middle Eastern countries, and even the term "Muslim Communist" has become part of the Soviet political jargon.

Soviet tactics employed in the Middle Eastern and Muslim countries are designed to fit each country's political situation. Sakharov explains that the Soviets will openly pursue friendly relations with a government but secretly back revolutionary groups intent on overthrowing that government. Those revolutionaries need not be Marxist—they can be Islamic or nationalistic—but they must be strongly anti-Western and, above all, show promise of being winners. The end justifying the means represents both the Communist and Islamic philosophies.

At the heart of the Soviet approach to Muslim countries is the propaganda that Islam and communism go hand-in-hand with building a new society. The Russians, with immense skill, manipulate Muslim emotions and faith to advance Soviet objectives. "The fanatics who were involved in the seizure of the Grand Mosque in Mecca," said Sakharov, "were among those I heard mentioned as part of the Soviet-sponsored People's Front of the Arabian Peninsula." The attack was blamed on the United States "through calumny spread rapidly throughout the Muslim world in typically efficient Soviet fashion." The Russians, contended Sakharov, used the assault to warn the Saudi Arabians that they were too favorable to Washington.

What Is At Stake

It is easy to understand why the Soviets are interested in manipulating Muslims. There are already approximately 700 million Muslims in the world, and Islamic leaders have as a goal some 1 billion followers of Allah by the year 2000.

The crucial factor in the Islamic-Communist alliance is the depth and enormity of anti-Western sentiment, the genuine and widespread hatred of the West, to be found in Islamic thought. It has taken root and flourished in the Muslim mind, and it has the potential for wild growth that might ultimately choke out all the West's best efforts in the Middle East.

The enmity the Muslim Arab world feels for the Christian West simply cannot be overestimated. No matter what other meeting points may seem to exist between Islam and communism, they are insignificant compared to their agreement on anti-Western sentiment.

This hatred of the infidel West, felt by so many

Muslim nations, is highly compatible with Qur'anic teaching, as we have seen. It is a very real danger to Western interests in the Middle East. And Russian intervention will only compound the problem.

If we are to hope for success in the Muslim world, especially the Arab world of the Middle East, we must understand this built-in enmity against the West in the Islamic mind. And we must understand how the Soviet Union exploits this sentiment to gain influence in the area at the West's expense. To understand that, we must realize that Islamic-Communist alliances have been formed in the past and can be formed in the future, and such alliances can only bode ill for the West.

The situation in the Middle East is not hopeless, however. We can and must build bridges to the Islamic world. At the same time, we must take steps to protect ourselves from deliberate attempts by Muslim extremists or potential extremists to use their investments in the West to harm our economies; we must walk a fine line between that need and the right of the Arabs, like any other foreign citizens, to invest in our economy. The next chapter offers a few ideas on how we should deal with the challenge of Islam.

8

Meeting the Challenge of Islam

In previous chapters we have discussed the great wealth of the Arab Muslims and the theology that motivates them in its use. We also have examined the Islamic principle of *jihad*, the ongoing holy war being fought for domination of the world. Divisions exist in Islam, and like any large group of people, it has its share of those who are concerned primarily with their own selfish interests.

But unlike other religions, Islam has as one of its most basic tenets the endless pursuit of *jihad*, and all true Muslims believe in it and pursue it to some extent or another. Thus, even so-called moderate Muslim leaders have this underlying determination in their dealings with the West. There is a large and growing radical element in Islam that is even more bent on holy war and would use more aggressively the Arabs' great oil supplies and wealth as weapons in that war.

Already the spread of Islam is impressive—and

threatening. The Muslims' well-funded evange-listic efforts have been so successful to date that Muslims expect to be dominant in Europe within the next few decades; furthermore they expect to become the world's largest religion in that same time period. Their growing influence is also evident here in the United States, where mosques are being erected in major cities, including a replica of the Dome of the Rock mosque (the original is in Jerusalem) going up in suburban Phoenix, Arizona. The history of Egypt gives us a good example of what happens to freedom in a country dominated by Islam.

Another potential danger is the high level of Islamic (primarily Arab) investment in the West, with the accompanying threat of economic disrup-tion. As we have seen earlier, Muslims do not hesitate to use their wealth to force conversion to Islam, or to force non-Muslims to comply with Islamic laws.

Faced with these facts, how do we react? How do we face the challenge of resurgent Islam and its invasion of the West? What measures would be appropriate and effective?

These are important questions, and no one, no matter how knowledgeable, has all the answers. Yet common sense and thorough historical exam-inations will prompt us to try to implement some simple, yet demanding, steps to avoid making the same mistake that others have made.

First, Westerners must seek to understand the

character and objectives of modern Islam and the serious threat it poses to their way of life. The ignorance and naiveté of most Westerners regarding Islam is alarming. Thus, the first thing the West must do is to become informed. People who are aware of the problem, especially Christians, must speak up in warning. Our governments, churches, and mass media need to be alerted to the truth of the situation. All individuals and groups who know what is happening share the responsibility for informing the Western public.

Second, the United States must tear itself loose from its dependency on OPEC oil. While the United States is the world's largest oil importer, the Soviet Union is the world's largest oil producer and is virtually energy self-sufficient. The United States is wrong if it assumes that OPEC countries would find it to their advantage to back the United States in a confrontation with the Russians. Any such assumption is fraught with danger.

There are some who continue to think America should not strive for energy independence. The cost would be too high, they say, and it would result in social disruption since it would reduce energy consumption substantially. Their approach to the problem is for Americans to do what they do best and let the Arabs do what they do best. The United States is more efficient at producing wheat and computers, their reasoning goes, and thus it would retain a bargaining leverage with OPEC.

That view, however, is too simplistic. It assumes

123

a world in which everything is measured in dollars and mathematical formulae. If that were reality, such a plan would make sense. But again, it illustrates Western naiveté about the religious dimension; Muslim states are made up of people who believe that to die in opposing the infidel is to earn oneself instant paradise.

America is not moving faster toward energy self-sufficiency because it does not take seriously the need to do so. The government's efforts to build a better energy base are being negated by special interests. As long as the short-term is the only point of focus in the United States' energy policy, the nation will not come close to energy independence. And, unfortunately, the short-term will continue to be the focus as long as America refuses to confront Islam for what it really is. Our nation will continue to dream of a relatively simple world where Muslims, Christians, and Jews share religious roots and, therefore, to a greater or lesser degree, will be able to live harmoniously with one another. But as long as "the House of Islam versus the House of War" mentality exists, there can be no peace between Muslims and their enemies.

Third, countries such as the United States must tighten foreign investment laws. The fear that Arab investors could bring down the American economy by yanking out their funds was the theme of the film *Rollover*. Imagine the chaos in American commercial centers if OPEC investors suddenly liquidated their assets, dumped their United States Treasury bills on the market, or transferred their liquid assets away from the United States. It is conceivable that extreme damage could be done to many sectors of the American economy by wild, dramatic financial manipulations by foreign investors.

Just how our investment laws should be modified is a matter for experts. But every nation has the right to protect its economy from manipulation by foreign investors, and safeguards are clearly needed.

On the other hand, everyone doing business with Muslim governments or individuals needs to make sure there are no religious strings attached to such dealings. Even then there are no foolproof ways to determine, for example, how a farmland or a bank is going to be used after it is sold. Westerners must never forget that there is more than economics involved whenever one does business with a Muslim.

Furthermore, we need to be as "wise as serpents" in the use of our resources. Let me illustrate. *Wall Street Journal* (December 30, 1982), in an article entitled "U.S. Set to Lease Federal Lands to Kuwait to Spare Foreign Investment Resources," reported that the federal government is ready to let Kuwait lease federal lands for energy and mineral development.

That same article indicated that once the administration permits Kuwait to acquire new federal leases, it is unlikely that other Middle East oil producers, looking for similar investments in the United States, would be denied access.

Based on the underlying ideology of Islam, the American government should seriously reconsider such action. It would open America to even more dangerous possibilities.

Islam spread throughout North Africa, Syria, Egypt, and Iran by the implementation of the concept of *jihad*. Deep into Africa and far into Asia, Islam spread by a different method: it spread through commerce and trading. Thus, when the editorial page of *Al Ahram* newspaper called for Arabs to use their muscle of $200 billion in the United States to get what they wanted, it became history repeating itself, rather than a mere prejudiced, alarmist misconception.

Fourth, the United States government must urge Islamic countries to allow all their citizens full human rights. It is illegal to be a citizen of certain Islamic countries, such as Saudi Arabia, unless one is a Muslim. Further, Christians, Jews, and members of other faiths are often (and in some nations always) forbidden to build churches.

The nations of the Christian West (the United States in particular) have declared themselves to be the protectors of the oppressed. How about using whatever influence they have to help the Christians, Jews, and other minorities in Egypt,

Syria, Ethiopia, Saudi Arabia, and many other countries?

Fifth, while in the West religious freedom is afforded all groups, including Muslims, Western governments must not allow antidemocratic Islamic laws to be incorporated into their bodies of law, which are based largely on Judeo-Christian values. In other words, Islamic freedom and growth in the West must not be allowed to be like "the camels in the tent," ultimately taking away the freedom of most.

Finally, Christianity must accept the challenge of Islam as a specifically religious challenge—in short, Christians need to practice what they preach. Western Christians boast that their societies are built on the foundation of Judeo-Christian ethics. If that is so, we should live both individually and collectively as Christians. We must learn the principle of loving those with whom we disagree theologically. On an international level, we must seek to love those who hate and condemn us. I am not suggesting that we should become weak or passive. Firmness and compassion are not mutually exclusive. We must speak and act with authority, yet without arrogance.

In a world of confusion, especially in the Middle East where growing pains are coupled with overt enmity between Muslims and Jews, the West needs to have clear and crisp objectives, firm and coherent policy. We need to be straightforward and honest even when we disagree. We need to construct our foreign policy on a firm basis of justice rather than on the basis of economic or political interests. Otherwise the Muslim world rightly will perceive the West as typically materialistic. This would only increase the danger of the flow of oil being disrupted.

The West must brace itself and plan ahead for still more resurgence of Islamic extremism. What we saw in Iran is merely the tip of the iceberg. As Muslim nations develop greater monetary power, adjustments and disturbances in society will become more evident and will overflow into political and religious life. As the Muslim nations, in general, and the Arab nations, in particular, try to express their independence in various ways, the West must convince them that we are friends, not foes.

The United States and Europe have given hundreds of millions of dollars in aid to several Muslim nations, but this fact often goes unnoticed by the general populace. The West should increase its positive propaganda to show the good things that Western nations are doing for the world, specifically the Muslim world.

Muslims have rejected adamantly the Western lifestyle because we all too often display only the most shallow and superficial aspects of our culture. Frankly, most Muslims are uninterested. And it is to their credit that they do not care for the Hollywood style with which we tend to display and represent ourselves. We must choose, rather, to show the Muslim world the true moral strength of the Western Christian heritage. It is our most valuable asset, and one we can keep only by using.